M000286598

STRAIGHT TO
THE TOP

Founded in 1807, John Wiley & Sons is the oldest independent publishing company in the United States. With offices in North America, Europe, Asia, and Australia, Wiley is globally committed to developing and marketing print and electronic products and services for our customers' professional and personal knowledge and understanding.

The Wiley CIO series provides information, tools, and insights to IT executives and managers. The products in this series cover a wide range of topics that supply strategic and implementation guidance on the latest technology trends, leadership, and emerging best practices.

Titles in the Wiley CIO series include:

The Agile Architecture Revolution: How Cloud Computing, REST-Based SOA, and Mobile Computing Are Changing Enterprise IT by Jason Bloomberg

Big Data, Big Analytics: Emerging Business Intelligence and Analytic Trends for Today's Businesses by Michele Chambers, Ambiga Dhiraj, and Michael Minelli

The Chief Information Officer's Body of Knowledge: People, Process, and Technology by Dean Lane

CIO Best Practices: Enabling Strategic Value with Information Technology by Joe Stenzel, Randy Betancourt, Gary Cokins, Alyssa Farrell, Bill Flemming, Michael H. Hugos, Jonathan Hujsak, and Karl D. Schubert

The CIO Playbook: Strategies and Best Practices for IT Leaders to Deliver Value by Nicholas R. Colisto

Enterprise IT Strategy, + Website: An Executive Guide for Generating Optimal ROI from Critical IT Investments by Gregory J. Fell

Executive's Guide to Virtual Worlds: How Avatars Are Transforming Your Business and Your Brand by Lonnie Benson

Innovating for Growth and Value: How CIOs Lead Continuous Transformation in the Modern Enterprise by Hunter Muller

IT Leadership Manual: Roadmap to Becoming a Trusted Business Partner by Alan R. Guibord

Managing Electronic Records: Methods, Best Practices, and Technologies by Robert F. Smallwood

On Top of the Cloud: How CIOs Leverage New Technologies to Drive Change and Build Value Across the Enterprise by Hunter Muller

Straight to the Top: CIO Leadership in a Mobile, Social, and Cloud-based World (Second Edition) by Gregory S. Smith

Strategic IT: Best Practices for Managers and Executives by Arthur M. Langer

Strategic IT Management: Transforming Business in Turbulent Times by Robert J. Benson

Transforming IT Culture: How to Use Social Intelligence, Human Factors, and Collaboration to Create an IT Department That Outperforms by Frank Wander

Unleashing the Power of IT: Bringing People, Business, and Technology Together by Dan Roberts

The U.S. Technology Skills Gap: What Every Technology Executive Must Know to Save America's Future by Gary Beach

STRAIGHT TO THE TOP

CIO LEADERSHIP IN A MOBILE, SOCIAL, AND CLOUD-BASED WORLD

SECOND EDITION

Gregory S. Smith

WILEY

Cover image: © 77studio/iStockphoto
Cover design: John Wiley & Sons, Inc.

Copyright © 2013 by John Wiley & Sons, Inc. All rights reserved.

Published by John Wiley & Sons, Inc., Hoboken, New Jersey.
First edition published by John Wiley & Sons, Inc. in 2006.
Published simultaneously in Canada.

No part of this publication may be reproduced, stored in a retrieval system, or transmitted in any form or by any means, electronic, mechanical, photocopying, recording, scanning, or otherwise, except as permitted under Section 107 or 108 of the 1976 United States Copyright Act, without either the prior written permission of the publisher, or authorization through payment of the appropriate per-copy fee to the Copyright Clearance Center, Inc., 222 Rosewood Drive, Danvers, MA 01923, (978) 750-8400, fax (978) 646-8600, or on the Web at www.copyright.com. Requests to the Publisher for permission should be addressed to the Permissions Department, John Wiley & Sons, Inc., 111 River Street, Hoboken, NJ 07030, (201) 748-6011, fax (201) 748-6008, or online at http://www.wiley.com/go/permissions.

Limit of Liability/Disclaimer of Warranty: While the publisher and author have used their best efforts in preparing this book, they make no representations or warranties with respect to the accuracy or completeness of the contents of this book and specifically disclaim any implied warranties of merchantability or fitness for a particular purpose. No warranty may be created or extended by sales representatives or written sales materials. The advice and strategies contained herein may not be suitable for your situation. You should consult with a professional where appropriate. Neither the publisher nor author shall be liable for any loss of profit or any other commercial damages, including but not limited to special, incidental, consequential, or other damages.

For general information on our other products and services or for technical support, please contact our Customer Care Department within the United States at (800) 762-2974, outside the United States at (317) 572-3993 or fax (317) 572-4002.

Wiley publishes in a variety of print and electronic formats and by print-on-demand. Some material included with standard print versions of this book may not be included in e-books or in print-on-demand. If this book refers to media such as a CD or DVD that is not included in the version you purchased, you may download this material at http://booksupport.wiley.com. For more information about Wiley products, visit www.wiley.com.

Library of Congress Cataloging-in-Publication Data:

Smith, Gregory S., 1963–
    Straight to the top : CIO leadership in a mobile, social, and cloud-based world / Gregory S. Smith. — Second Edition.
        pages cm
    Includes index.
    ISBN 978-1-118-39003-0 (hbk.) — ISBN 978-1-118-42079-9 (ePDF) — ISBN 978-1-118-59564-0 (Mobi) — ISBN 978-1-118-41746-1 (ePub) — ISBN 978-1-118-63422-6 (O-book)
    1. Chief information officers — Vocational guidance.   2. Information technology—Management—Vocational guidance.   3. Information resources management—Vocational guidance.   I. Title.
    HD30.2.S629 2013
    658.4'038—dc23

                                                                2012048297

Printed in the United States of America

10 9 8 7 6 5 4 3 2 1

To all of the IT professionals—inside organizations and within supporting vendors—who make this industry so exciting. Keep driving innovation and change every day.

Also, to the executive recruiters who are so often instrumental in the recruitment and placement of today's CIOs and supporting executives. Thanks for all your hard work.

And, finally, to my family for their continued support and patience during the research and writing of this book.

CONTENTS

PREFACE

For the past decade and a half, I have had the luxury of serving as the chief information officer (CIO) for some wonderful global organizations. Before accepting my first CIO post at the World Wildlife Fund (WWF), I had the privilege of serving as a principal consultant for one of the most prestigious consulting firms in the world, as an information technology (IT) director at a Fortune 200 financial services firm, as a defense IT consultant, and as an adjunct professor at one of the top 20 American universities.

The role of IT has been changing for decades and is changing still. Looking back, I reflect on the days of centralized computing on mainframes, client-server technology, web 1.0, telecommunications advances, and mobile computing gains—most recently, the significant advances in smart phone and tablet technologies. Today we have new drivers for change. We are heavily leveraging cloud technology, social networking, advanced telecommunication and wireless technologies, the virtualization of everything technical, and the advancement of consumer devices in the corporate world. As a result, the role of the CIO in any organization continues to be demanding and requires solid technical skills, business acumen, and exceptional communication skills to properly succeed.

Preparing for the CIO role takes careful planning. Staying in that role takes continued education in modern technologies, trust from your staff and other C-level executives, and the ability to deliver results at the lowest cost possible.

In 2006, I published *Straight to the Top: Becoming a World-Class CIO*. The book was intended to serve two main goals: (1) to help nonexecutive IT professionals plan their ascension to the top echelons of IT and, if lucky, their appointment to the CIO role, and (2) to assist sitting CIOs with best-practice information and shared knowledge from a variety of seasoned professionals (CIOs, executive recruiters, and top IT advisory research firms) to become better IT leaders.

Straight to the Top: CIO Leadership in a Mobile, Social, and Cloud-based World continues the journey of educating today's IT leaders and tomorrow's successors. Thus, my goal in this book is to help sitting CIOs, aspiring CIOs, and other business professionals to understand the drivers, complexities, and positioning of IT in the business world today so that as an industry and as leaders in that industry, we become better.

The Target Audience

Straight to the Top: CIO Leadership in a Mobile, Social, and Cloud-based World is targeted at IT and business professionals who aspire to land senior management positions in IT or who desire to become top IT resources in their organizations. The book expands on the first edition and focuses on technology and business drivers that are changing the landscape of IT today.

Academic institutions that offer programs and degrees (undergraduate and graduate) in information systems, computer science, and IT management, along with their faculty, should benefit from this book by using it to augment the content of their courses with real-world skills that can propel their students to reach the upper echelons of technology management.

Today's successful technology professionals need to have solid IT acumen, business skills, strong communication skills, and a willingness to embrace the changing landscape in business and technology. Mobile, social, and cloud solutions are here to stay. They are getting more mature and are permeating the marketplace even as I write this. The nonbusiness consumer is having a profound effect on technology in organizations today. Trends in consumer technology and social media are blurring the lines between traditional IT management and governance and the frameworks required today. They are requiring top IT leaders to take another look and reshape their organizations to accommodate these technologies and drivers.

Straight to the Top: CIO Leadership in a Mobile, Social, and Cloud-based World describes why the role of the CIO is changing and what to expect in the future. It introduces topics beyond those in the first edition to help IT professionals govern their technical environments. The readers will get an expanded view from a diverse group of executive recruiters to see exactly what qualities, skills, and experiences quality search firms are seeking in CIO candidates. I compare and contrast the data in the first edition with the data in this edition. This book explores in more depth the social and technical drivers for IT change, including social media, mobile computing, and cloud technologies; it recommend how to navigate the C-suite; and it concludes with what's next for CIOs after mastering the technology leadership role.

The Approach

The information and recommendations presented in this book come from a variety of sources: (1) advisory research and case studies, (2) interviews with a diverse range of CIO experts and seasoned IT leaders, (3) interviews with a variety of executive recruiting firms, and (4) my own experiences in both planning for my first CIO role and serving as a CIO for more than a decade. The expert CIOs surveyed for this book come from a diverse group of organizations that represent a large cross-section of industries and sectors, including academia, nonprofit, retail, technology services, pharmaceuticals, and financial services. The CIO and executive recruiting expertise and input are derived from regional, national, and international experience and depth.

Part I focuses on the drivers and changes affecting information technology and the role of the CIO. Expanding on the first edition, I examine additional best practices of governance, standards, and service levels and explore how to interact, advise, and educate other C-level executives in the pursuit of IT excellence.

Part II builds on the drivers and recommendations discussed in the first half of the book and homes in on several key topics relevant to today, including cloud computing, the consumerization of IT, and social media and networking. The readers will get an updated view from top executive recruiters on what they are looking for when hiring for senior IT leadership positions today.

ACKNOWLEDGMENTS

I'd like to thank the folks at Forrester Research, specifically George Colony, for his continued support of research and IT advisory services that greatly contributed to the success of this book.

I'd also like to thank my CIO peer group of IT leaders and executives for their contributions and insights. Their input lends legitimacy and credibility by providing real-world examples of challenges and solutions to today's complex IT and business environment.

In addition, the information and insight provided by my IT executive recruiting professionals is priceless. I hope it helps the readers with their next career moves.

Finally, but with no less importance, thanks to my editors, Tim Burgard and Stacey Rivera, at John Wiley & Sons and to the many literary professionals on the Wiley team who helped bring this book to fruition.

PART ONE

Key Change Drivers and Trends Impacting the CIO Role Today

CHAPTER 1

Why the Role of the CIO Continues to Change

**

The only way of finding the limits of the possible is by going beyond them into the impossible.

—Arthur C. Clark[1]

I am honored to have the opportunity to write the second edition of *Straight to the Top* for several reasons. First, the information technology (IT) market continues to be robust and a constantly changing canvas that allows vendors, consumers, and IT professionals the opportunity to paint their masterpieces with different technical tools and colors.

Second, my editors at John Wiley & Sons and I saw the market opportunity to update the original text, and they had confidence in me to write the succeeding volume in a way that would assist and educate IT and business professionals on the rise.

Third, I am concerned that the chief information officer (CIO) role may be evolving to a dangerously nontechnical role that relies more on business acumen and less on IT experience and knowledge. A less technical CIO role has been a topic in a variety of media outlets for years now, and the volume seems to be rising. In a recent interview with a major media player, the journalist asked me my thoughts on whether the CIO role still needed to be technical. The interviewer suggested rotating other C-level executives through the CIO role on a six-month basis as a way to interject other business knowledge into the role. He indicated that some organizations were experimenting with this unique technique.

When asked whether I supported this process, I answered the question with a resounding *no*. I went on to suggest that it wasn't a good idea to extend that concept and rotate the CIO through other C-level positions, including chief financial officer (CFO) and chief marketing officer (CMO). Can you imagine what would happen to a CIO rotating through a CFO role during the certification of year-end financials—especially if there are issues and audit management comments? The answer is the possibility of prison.

Regarding the skills that CIOs need today, let me be crystal clear. The CIO *must* have technical knowledge (practical and theoretical) *in addition to* solid business skills in order to be able to succeed in today's complex environments and beyond. I have met many CIOs who are well received in the marketplace and who are accomplished in the delivery of several large and complex projects but who lack the technical skills and the trust of their own staffs. In the first edition of this book, I cited a CIO research report finding that more than 40 percent of IT staff members surveyed thought that their CIOs were not technically savvy enough about their companies' technologies to lead their respective departments.[2] Today's CIOs need to be technically savvy *and* business savvy.

Let me be crystal clear with my next statement as well. CIOs throughout this and the next decade need to be IT leaders with tremendous business *and* technical skills. They need to understand wireless technologies, security, cloud computing, social networking, virtualization, and business intelligence in addition to the "softer" skills like vendor and contract management, communication, financial management, and IT governance. I still believe that those experiences—combined with the right academic mix of a bachelor's degree in computer science, engineering, or information systems and a master's degree in business—form the killer combination. I'll explore this topic more in Chapter 6, where regional, national, and international executive recruiters weigh in on the skills and experience needed by today's IT leaders.

IT leaders who have great business acumen and experience will undoubtedly need to rely on their subordinates or outside consulting experts for technical skills and IT know-how, but business-only CIOs run the risk of relying on them too much. Concepts in IT networking and operations as well as mobile and cloud technologies—including significant changes in integration technology, software development, enterprise applications, and security—are all fairly technical components inside IT. I believe that CIOs with solid technical grounding are better able to rally their IT departments, gain their respect and trust, and appropriately build a successful multiyear strategy that includes a comprehensive and shared discussion with their subordinates, but not one that is dictated by them due to the CIOs' lack of technical grounding.

An analogy that I used in the first edition stated it clearly and looked at the question of expertise from a different perspective and discipline. Does a CFO need to be well grounded in both financial management and accounting principles? Undoubtedly, yes. Similarly, the CIO needs to be technical in his or her role. Thus, CIO leaders today need to be the full package: savvy in technology and seasoned business professionals.

Since I last penned *Straight to the Top*, I've been busy expanding my career, building my knowledge on the many changing technologies affecting

IT executives today, and learning more about the businesses of the organizations in which I've had the honor of serving. These three accomplishments in continuing education are no small feat. As of this writing, social media is alive and well and becoming more and more important to the CIO strategy every day. No longer is social media just a way for staff members who are bored out of their minds at work to waste time chatting with friends online. Facebook, Twitter, and other technologies are vibrant, are expanding at a mind-boggling pace, and are causing a major paradigm shift in IT strategies today.

In addition, the cloud is no longer an experiment, but rather a viable business model and technical opportunity for organizations looking to roll out applications faster and with more fault tolerance and expandability. Consumer devices are invading organizations at an alarming rate, multiplying with vendor and model variations, and providing throbbing headaches for IT professionals across the globe who adopt them. Old-school technocrats are used to *controlled* environments and systems. Modern-day CIOs need to embrace and manage a changing technology that includes tablets, new smartphones, social networking (including via mobile), and collaboration in the cloud. These are all examples of disruptive technologies that are maturing and causing CIOs to rethink their strategies and governance models.

Consumer tools like Apple's iPad, Google's Nexus 7, Amazon's Kindle, Microsoft's Surface tablet, and Samsung's Galaxy are pushing the limits of tablet computing and moving more IT organizations into a decentralized heterogeneous mobile environment. This, of course, is in addition to the plethora of personal digital assistants (PDAs) on the market and the behind-the-scenes war of the mobile device operating systems. IT standards and governance are being tested every day with new technology releases and consumer adoption of these devices. Bring your own device (BYOD) to work is having a profound effect on IT departments today. I'll have more to say about that in a subsequent chapter, but the bottom line is that the consumerization of IT is happening, and we can't stop it. Those who put their heads in the sand and ignore this trend may be hailed as security hawks, but they won't be loved by the employees of the organization, many of whom are members of Generations X and Y.

Gone are the days of Internet Explorer–only or –dominant browsers, BlackBerry-only business-grade smartphones, and the fat personal computer that stored all programs, data, and processing power on a synchronized platform of local client machines and centralized servers. Nope—we're in for a new ride now. Organizations are deploying cloud-based and mobile applications at breakneck speeds. The integration of data between cloud technologies and on-premise systems is also changing, adding layers of complexity, especially in terms of stability and security.

I recently spoke at a CIO event in Canada about the changing IT landscape and the drivers that are pushing CIOs to reevaluate their strategies.

Although many CIOs in the audience communicated a solid understanding of these drivers—with several able to discuss their strategies in support of mobile, cloud, and social technology—there were a couple who had not developed strategies in one or two of the shifting drivers affecting the IT industry. This perplexed me a bit, but then it hit me months later, when I was in a completely different geographical part of the world.

CIOs have been trying for so long to control their environments through classic governance models with nonflexible standards that some of them have actually been able to stave off disruptive technologies likes the ones affecting the marketplace today. I've spoken to many CIOs who block social media web sites from their staff members at work, block access to personal e-mail, don't allow online shopping during business hours, and don't support or allow personal devices on their networks. For the sake of firm control, these CIOs have sacrificed opportunities for both professional and business growth.

Many of the technologies driving change and innovation today in the marketplace may help our teams be more collaborative, open, and remote or mobile in the goals of driving revenue and improving customer support. Thus, it's time for today's IT executives to adapt or die and for the next generation of IT leaders to pressure the existing leadership to improve.

I realized shortly after the conversations in Canada that CIOs in India are not as fluent with the new integration technologies that enable cloud-to-cloud and cloud-to-premise integration. In China, CIOs are light on virtualization technology usage and strategies. Technology is changing fast enough that different parts of the globe are better than others at adopting newer strategies and technologies. And in many cases, slower adoption is a form of risk mitigation.

The State of the CIO

A recent *CIO* magazine article posed the question of whether IT is facing a leadership crisis. According to Aaron Cowan, who leads recruiting for the executive search firm Marlin Hawk, "The talent exists in the market. The world creates the leaders it needs."[3]

Next-generation CIOs will come from a variety of sources, including the following two:

1. A variety of business units (marketing, human resources, finance, sales).
2. Information technology departments (software development, Web and e-business, IT operations).

According to Forrester Research's Khalid Kark, "We're starting to see more and more CIOs who are not traditional technologists. We estimate anywhere from 60 to 65 percent of CIOs still have a strong technology background." And Mark Polansky of executive search firm Korn Ferry stated, "There are some non-IT people who become CIOs. They are the exceptions and not the rule."[4]

IT resources in the United States, sometimes in the higher ranks, are not as plentiful as they once were. Computer science programs are cranking out fewer top candidates than they did a decade ago. According to Katrina Lane, chief technology officer (CTO) of Caesar's Entertainment, an $8.8 billion casino, the company is having a difficult time bringing on board several senior IT staff. Because of a difficult economy and reduced mobility for relocation, she explained, "they can't get rid of their houses, and you end up having a smaller pool of people to draw from." Companies that can't find the right top IT talent may have a harder time growing. According to Tim Campos, director of IT at Facebook, "We can't hire fast enough. It's very difficult for us to find the best talent."[5]

The most recent research from *CIO* magazine, drawn from the annual State of the CIO survey, found that 82 percent of the 596 IT leaders surveyed "expect the global recession will have a negative impact on their organization within the next three years."[6] Given the numerous public attacks and theft of data in both small and large organizations, 69 percent are expecting a security-related issue within the next three years.

Fewer CIOs report to their chief executive officers (CEO), a downward trend in the past four years; as of 2012, only 38 percent were reporting directly to the CEO (see Exhibit 1.1). In addition, *CIO* magazine reported that CIOs reporting to the CFOs is on the rise, up slightly to 23 percent.[7]

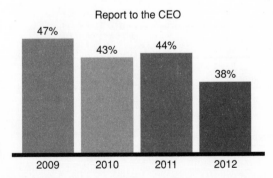

Fewer CIOs report to the CEO. Twenty-three percent of respondents now report to the CFO, up slightly from 20 percent in 2011 and 19 percent in 2010.

Report to the CEO

47%   43%   44%   38%

2009   2010   2011   2012

Exhibit 1.1   Strategic Access

To me and to many of the colleagues I've discussed the reporting trend with, the results are indicative of stress caused by the end of the U.S. recession, the start of a recession in Europe, a slowdown in China's growth, and the effects of interrelated commerce across the globe. I've been through four recessions in my career. A consistent outcome of each one was more reliance on the CFO for managing the organization's investments and expenses. I see no difference now in the driver for this year's trend of an increasing number of CIOs reporting to the CFOs.

IT organizations are increasingly under pressure to deliver during uneven economic times. The perceptions of their business stakeholders have come into play more with this year's State of the CIO survey. Even though the strategic contributions from most CIOs have grown in recent years, "57 percent of surveyed CIOs believe they are perceived as service providers or technology collaborators." Only 7 percent are perceived as "game changers," 30 percent as "IT partners," 27 percent as "service providers," and 21 percent as a cost center providing no appreciated enterprise value or misunderstood as a cost center as a whole (see Exhibit 1.2). An interesting anecdote is that CIOs reporting to CEOs is highly correlated with the CIOs being perceived as business savvy. Those lucky executives make up 60 percent of the technology leaders, compared to 38 percent with less perceived business value outside IT.[8]

Despite all this bad news, there is a bit of good news: 66 percent of the IT leaders surveyed sit on the management committee (see Exhibit 1.3).[9] Tenure is also on the rise, with an average tenure of five years and four months.[10]

How you think business leaders perceive IT

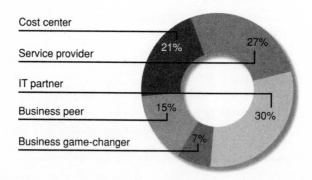

Cost center

Service provider

IT partner

Business peer

Business game-changer

21% 27% 30% 15% 7%

Exhibit 1.2 The Way Others See You

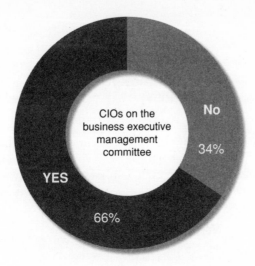

Exhibit 1.3   Do You Have a Seat at the Table?

So what does this all mean for the future of IT and CIO leadership trends? According to the survey, the CIOs felt much better about their ability to meet their current year goals: 63 percent reported having a good year, 37 percent reported a challenge, and 1 percent were not sure. Regarding the organization's business outlook, the statistics were practically reversed: 65 percent saw a challenging year, and only 34 percent had a positive attitude for a good year (see Exhibit 1.4).[11]

How Important Are Core Technology Skills?

Keen IT skills are very important today in order to be successful as a CIO. Some of the research in the market today indicates that technology skills for CIOs rank as a much lower priority than business acumen and communication skills, which are at the top of the list of must-have skills. Many CIOs whom I've spoken with over the years and encountered in peer meetings, at conferences, and on conference calls still do not appear to have sufficient knowledge of many of the components driving IT today; they appear to rely heavily on their trusted subordinates to give them advice and help them make technical decisions.

This was evident in my recent trip and presentation to a group of CIOs in North America. Although the majority of the IT leaders I spoke with had solid business plans and were investing in many of the technologies that are

The Outlook for 2012

Your organization's business outlook   Your IT team's ability to hit its goals

Good year

Challenging year 34%

Not sure

65%

1%

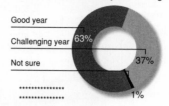

Good year

Challenging year 63%

Not sure

37%

1%

What's Driving Change

You say these trends will have the most profound
effect on the CIO role in the future:

Technology as a service (cloud)

Mobility   34%

Ubiquinous data (big data)   25%

Consumerization of desktops and devices

Social media and networking   11%   18%

13%

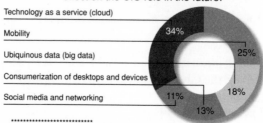

What You Want to Do

Favorite ways to spend your
time in the next 3 to 5 years:

Driving business innovation

Identifying opportunities for
competitive differentiation

Developing and refining
business strategy

Least favorite ways to spend
your time in the next 3 to 5 years:

Managing IT crises

Negotiating with IT vendors

Controlling costs

Exhibit 1.4   What the Future Holds
Source: www.cio.com, December 15, 2011, and January 1, 2012

rapidly penetrating into the marketplace today, a few had no real strategy for leveraging technologies like cloud computing or social media and still relied heavily on subordinates to do the IT heavy lifting.

During two other speaking engagements—one in South Asia, and the other in China—I also noted a lack of technical knowledge associated with today's trending technologies, including cloud computing, cloud integration technology, social media, and, in some cases, virtualization. Several of the Indian and Chinese CTOs and CIOs I spoke with were unfamiliar with new cloud-based integration technologies from recognizable vendors such as Dell, Software AG, and IBM. What became obvious to me as I researched this book is that the adoption rate of leading technologies *does* vary greatly across the globe, and it is often correlated in some way to technology spending trends in regions and countries. North America and Europe typically lead the globe on technology innovation, but that landscape is starting to change.

Relying solely on technical subordinates can be a dangerous decision for today's IT leaders, mainly because CIO subordinates will in many ways determine how successful the CIO is. What if a subordinate ill advises a CIO and the outcome of a major initiative is a flop? Worse yet, what if revenue or customer support is affected? This can sometimes result in the CIO losing his or her job. As a CIO, I can't imagine leading a team of IT professionals without having solid technical skills. I would never put my career in the hands of subordinates by relying on them to make decisions on strategy and technology that I am responsible for. CIOs need to have modern-day core technology skills and experience *in addition to* many other "soft" skills, including business acumen in the sectors in which their organizations reside. CIOs need to be the *whole* package.

In the first edition, I noted the following important IT skills for CIOs:

- Applications and architecture alternatives
- Database management systems
- Networking and wireless technologies
- Collaboration systems
- Security

As a result of spending forecasts and the 2012 State of the CIO survey of IT leaders, the technical skills to have now are the following:

- Cloud computing and virtualization
- Integration technologies (middleware)
- Mobile devices and wireless technologies
- Telecommunications

- A renewed focus on security—including data loss and prevention
- Big data, analytics, and the integration of business intelligence
- Social media and networking

In the first edition, I highlighted an architecture commonly found inside an organization's data center or maintained by a hosting partner. Exhibit 1.5 displays the components that were likely to be found in a data center six or more years ago. To fully understand this architecture, CIOs need to under-stand networking concepts; database knowledge and integration techniques; clustering; and operating system scale and performance. This architecture is still used by technology professionals today.

Fast forward to today. The architectures of today include many compo-nents used six years ago, but they expand to include additional integration technologies and often rely on external public and private cloud computing solution providers and virtualization. A common change to the architecture depicted in Exhibit 1.5 is the use of virtualization technologies in place of dedicated servers. Virtualization offers many advantages to prior data center and system configuration. Some examples of virtualization technology ben-efits are (1) a higher utilization of server capacity (density), often resulting in an overall lower total cost of ownership, (2) reduced energy consumption, (3) an increased fault tolerance of server resources, (4) faster provisioning of server resources, and (5) major improvements in disaster recovery planning and execution as a result of being able to replicate data and systems across data centers. More and more CIOs are incorporating cloud computing into their enterprise architectures. I'll discuss cloud computing in much more detail in Chapter 7.

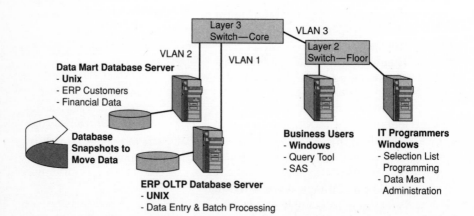

Exhibit 1.5   Sample IT OLTP to Decision Support Architecture

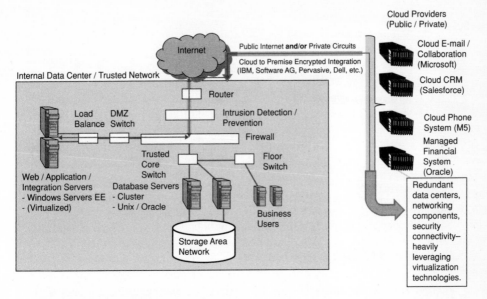

Exhibit 1.6   Cloud/Integration Architecture

Exhibit 1.6 highlights the complexity and integration between on-premise data centers and cloud provider data centers. This technique also brings in a whole new component of vendor contract negotiation that requires CIOs to focus on system uptime, the provisioning of servers, the use and cost of disk space, service level agreements (SLAs), security, data integration, and penalties for failed SLAs. The more CIOs leverage cloud computing solutions, the more integration that's typically required and the more we need to pay attention to the services and SLAs the cloud vendors provide.

Virtualization has also moved from servers to many other networking and client computing devices. It's common for a cloud provider to leverage virtualization technology to provision load balancers, firewalls, intrusion detection and prevention devices, and even switches. While virtualization technologies are mature in the data center, they are still evolving on the client side—specifically, the user computer or laptop. The increase in user mobility is pushing the limits on virtualization technologies applied to individual computers, mainly by the requirement to work offline and away from the corporate network. Vendors such as Citrix and EMC/VMWare are making progress solving the offline virtualization need and are expected to reach critical mass with regard to maturity in the next few years.

Exhibit 1.7 is an example of a green IT architecture, in which energy use and server utilization (via higher density) is achieved through virtualization technologies and blade computing. Some SAN disk systems today incorporate smart

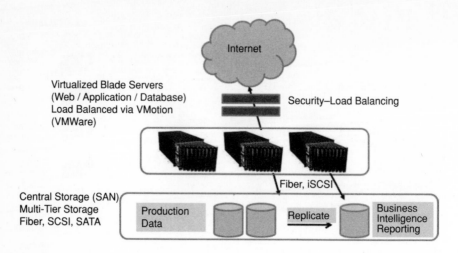

Exhibit 1.7 Sample Green IT Architecture

energy-sensitive technologies built in to automate the migration of data from high-speed, high-energy drives to low-cost, low-energy drives based on usage.

To round out this introductory chapter, I asked my distinguished CIO/executive panel two questions about the CIO role today and why it has changed in recent years. Their insights and responses are listed in the CIO survey below.

CIO SURVEY

What are the top three roles of the CIO today?

- Managing and leveraging technical innovation to enhance business and create opportunity.

- Providing prudence and guidance in a culture of transformation for businesses and customers.

- Encouraging management and mitigation of risk upstream and downstream by fostering a hardened and crisis-resistant business ecosystem across our supply chain—from source to sale, concept to distribution—in an environment of change.

—*Martin Gomberg, former CIO; SVP and Global Director, Business Protection, A&E Networks*

- Building an ecosystem that allows us to bring our clients and customers closer to our organizations.
- Being entrepreneurial—being nimble with changing landscapes (regulation, market changes, new lines of business).
- Building a global workforce.

—*Sanjay Khatnani, President, J2 Solutions*

- Knowing how to use IT as a lever for transformation.
- Being able to invest in an optimal and rigorous manner while ensuring that IT is used appropriately.
- Optimizing the management of know-how and expertise in a climate of manpower and resource scarcity.

—*Denis Garon, Associate with the Secretary of the Chief Information Secretariat of the Council of Treasury*

- Being a trusted business counselor and partner. Credibility is established through relationship.
- Being a business change agent.
- Marketing, publicizing, and selling technology solutions to internal customers.

—*Joel Schwalbe, CIO, CNL Financial Group*

Why has the CIO role changed in the last three to five years?

- Technology advancements are simplifying the lower layers in the technology stack (infrastructure in the enterprise architecture and up).
- Cloud computing is shifting the focus on solution delivery away from traditional IT delivery and putting more capabilities in the hands of business leaders.
- Financially, IT will never see spending like we did during the Y2K, dotcom boom. Tight budgets will remain for the foreseeable future.
- Consumer and employee expectations are blurring. Personal computing and computing done in business transactions and at work are no longer acceptable to have outdated and cumbersome solutions for commerce when people are used to simple, elegant solutions in all other situations.

(Continued)

CIO SURVEY (*Continued*)

- The IT debt of the past 10 to 15 years of solutions remains unpaid and is severely hampering the ability of most corporate shops.
—*Peter Classon, Partner, LiquidHub Inc.*

- I think the importance of data has made the CIO role more of a transformation role than it has ever been. Data analytics, social media, and data mash-ups can provide the information organizations need to make strategic change and progress as never before.

- The professionalism and expertise of cyber criminals has forced the CIO to take on a leadership role in the protection of digital assets.

- The advent of SaaS, IaaS, and cloud-based solutions has allowed the CIO to move from a developer of solutions to an integrator of key solutions, which allows an investment in the outcomes rather than the development. CIOs need to be more focused on the outcomes and less on how the outcomes were developed.
—*Ed Anderson, International CIO, World Vision International*

- There is much more emphasis on relationships and business and less on technology—at least, if you want to be successful.

- I focus on solutions to the business problems; whether they incorporate technology or not is irrelevant.

- Business expectations have changed. The status quo is unacceptable—CIOs must always look to identify and take advantage of concepts that will lead to revenue enhancement, risk mitigation, or efficiency gains. IT departments are either viewed as a bunch of "order takers" or considered a strategic element in the business, an extension that ultimately makes the business more competitive.
—*Joel Schwalbe, CIO, CNL Financial Group*

- There is more of a focus on economics (revenue and cost) and risk mitigation.
—*David Swartz, CIO, American University*

What Did I Do to Prepare?

I started out my career by obtaining an undergraduate degree in computer science with a minor in business from the best program I could get into. It turned out that when I graduated from the University of Maryland at College Park, it had the seventh best computer science program in the United States. In addition, Maryland's business program ranked in the top 25. After working several years as a programmer in a consulting firm, where I proactively shared knowledge with coworkers and worked toward being part of a team effort, I became a team leader, then a manager. Becoming a manager gave me oversight over larger projects and consulting engagements.

I enrolled in a graduate technical MBA degree program at Johns Hopkins University to expand my business knowledge and gain additional skills for IT oversight and management. In the early 1990s, I moved to a large financial services Fortune 200 firm to expand my skills and work with larger, more complex systems, including financial systems, real-time trading applications, complex telecommunications delivery systems (terrestrial and satellite for financial feeds), Internet-enabled applications, database management systems, and decision support and business intelligence systems. In 1992, at the age of 29, I published my first article in *LAN Times* magazine.

I bring up my educational and work past because it reiterates a key component in this chapter: that the IT industry is never static and thus requires continuing education to stay ahead. Education to me comes in many forms, not just through academic institutions and degrees. Getting certified and taking continuing education courses in the technologies your company is investing in will pay huge dividends toward your future career. Keep an eye on what other companies and industries are investing in as well. They usually indicate the leading edge of technology investments and thus the technologies being used to drive innovation in the marketplace.

Today, my journey of learning and sharing knowledge continues. I've been fortunate to have authored four books, to have given dozens of presentations around the globe, and to have written many articles. On the continuing education front, I continue to educate myself via books, vendor demos, and technical training sessions to stay up to date on technologies and trends.

I have forced myself to adapt to the changing trends and technologies that many of us are working on today. While adapting to changes, I've completely redesigned my approach to security and integration as a result of the changing technology landscape and tools. I encourage other IT executives to learn a bit from the next generation of IT leaders who are helping to drive changes in IT through their adoption and use of disruptive technologies. As a collective group of professionals, we must push ourselves outside the control conundrum and comfort zone and adapt to these drivers and new technologies. The drivers and changes will affect the future, whether we like it not. Embrace them or die trying.

In coordination with one of the CIO survey questions, I was recently asked, "What is the most important skill for CIOs today?" After a long pause, I answered, "The ability to say no." This does not mean that I'm a CIO who subscribes to a negative approach or repressive responses that include "It can't happen," "We can't do it," "We don't have enough staff or money," and so on. What it means is that successful CIOs figure out what they can do and what they cannot do with a limited amount of money and resources (internal and consulting).

The CIOs who are successful know their limitations, as so aptly described by the great Clint Eastwood in *Dirty Harry*, the classic police thriller of the 1970s. San Francisco's finest, Harry Callahan, had a gun pointed at a criminal who just moments earlier had been on the run, fleeing from the chasing officer. When the criminal was cornered, Callahan said to him, "You've got to ask yourself one question: 'Do I feel lucky?' Well, do ya, punk?" After a brief moment (and, I'm sure, a Hollywood-inspired reflection), the criminal lunged for Callahan's gun. In response, Dirty Harry shot and killed the varmint. In the movie *Magnum Force*, Eastwood had the following poetic advice for his lieutenant: "A man's got to know his limitations." This is my IT poetic moment and translation regarding what CIOs must know to be successful in this increasingly mobile, social, and consumer device-driven world.

You should know the following:

- Your project pipeline and change effect on the existing portfolio of initiatives.
- Your staff's capabilities and availability.
- Your customer's needs, personalities, and business drivers. Not all are up front.
- Your vendor's products and capabilities. CIOs need to be able to cut through the marketing hype and quickly get to product capabilities in a short amount of time. Time is money for today's IT executives, and most simply don't have a lot to spare.
- Your consultant's capabilities and loyalty. Some may be spies. Others may be looking for a permanent job and lose focus on the engagement at hand.
- Your business peers, demands, needs, and interworkings. I weight this item higher than most of the others.

In closing, and to reword my initial response of no: CIOs today must be well versed in knowing their limitations, must know their business customers well and build trusting relationships, must know and trust their staff's expertise and instincts, and respond yes to the difficult questions in their organization. Yes, we can add this new project to the portfolio. Yes, we can meet your needs and time lines and stay on budget. Saying yes today requires noting what it takes to get there—specifically, the exact resources we need to meet an objective and the range of time and money required to meet the demand. That's the new way of saying yes. The qualification of what it takes to do what is needed.

Recommendations

I advise professionals who aspire to become CIOs—as well as sitting CIOs, currently in the role—not lose focus on the core technology skills that are necessary to run a world-class IT team. Individuals today are more in charge of their careers and planning than ever before. Planning your career earlier while setting clear, measured, and obtainable goals can get you to where you want to be, if you are persistent and patient. The following recommendations are designed for today's IT professionals to adapt to the changes in technology and business culture to be successful:

- Volunteer to join or lead project teams where you can gain additional IT skills and business knowledge.
- Keep learning. For younger professionals, augment your undergraduate degree with an advanced degree and focus on courses that will enhance your ability to lead teams and drive strategy. I prefer traditional nonprofit educational institutions over the growing for-profit colleges and universities, most of whom offer primarily online degrees. If you do elect to continue your formal education, get into the best school that you can afford. Reputation matters.
- Strengthen your business knowledge. Meet with business peers for lunch or brown-bag sessions to increase your knowledge of the industry your organization represents.
- Take continuing education courses and obtain certification in the latest technologies being used in your organization. If possible, get up to speed on the latest security trends and technologies, social media, cloud computing, integration technologies, and the management of consumer technologies.
- Add consulting experience to your resume. Consulting engagements offer a unique way to learn what businesses need and how to deliver value from an entirely different perspective. The experience is almost required for CIOs today. The executives I know who have consulting experience are better negotiators with their vendors.

- Get engaged with vendors with whom you do business (or may do business with in the future) to learn new technologies and/or processes that can be applied to today's complex business challenges.
- Conduct and attend brown-bag sessions for cross-training and information sharing of technology and business topics in your department and across other departments.
- Attend vendor seminars and demonstration sessions on the latest and relevant technology topics.
- Read periodicals and other publications to gain additional insights and perspectives on executive leadership and strategic planning.
- Conduct research, when applicable, and review the best practices and vendor solutions needed to solve real business problems. IT advisory firms like Forrester Research and Gartner have great analysts and super research across a wide-ranging set of technologies, vendors, and strategies.
- Share ideas and best practices with your peers and subordinates. Create a culture of learning.

In closing, CIOs with strong and *current* technical skills, business acumen, a drive to win, and an attitude of sharing will add tremendous value to an organization and grow. For those still on the rise to the CIO spot, start doing what it takes for the next job above yours. You're likely to get promoted faster if you demonstrate the skills that are required in the position above yours. Keep doing this all the way to the top.

Notes

1. Arthur C. Clark, Inspirational Quotes, www.inspirational-quotes.info/motivational-quotes .html (accessed on July 28, 2012).
2. Lorraine Cosgrove Ware, "What Do You Think of Your CIO?", *CIO Research Reports*, September 15, 2003, www2.cio.com/research/surveyreport.cfm?id=63 (accessed February 26, 2005).
3. Meridith Levinson, "CIO Role: Is IT Facing a Leadership Crisis?", *CIO*, October 21, 2011, www.cio.com/article/print/692324 (accessed July 20, 2012).
4. Ibid.
5. Kim S. Nash, "Business Disconnect," *CIO*, January 1, 2012, 45.
6. "*CIO* Magazine 2012 State of the CIO Survey—Executive Summary," *CIO*, January 1, 2012, 1.
7. Ibid., 31.
8. Ibid., 1
9. Ibid., 31.
10. Ibid., 34.
11. Ibid.

CHAPTER 2

Technologies and Trends Driving Today's IT Innovation

The future belongs to those who believe in the beauty of their dreams.
—ELEANOR ROOSEVELT[1]

Technologies that are driving innovation today are typically reflected in what organizations are spending their technology funds on—both in the current year and projected into the future. According to *CIO* magazine's "State of the CIO 2012" research report, larger companies are spending less as a measure of revenue at 3.7 percent. Small and medium-size organizations are spending between 4 and 6 percent of revenue (see Exhibit 2.1). Breaking down the numbers by industry, we see that high technology and utilities lead the way, with the highest percent of revenue spending at 7.6 percent. This year's average is 4.7 percent. Health care, manufacturing, and retail bring up the rear, with the lowest percentages of spending, at 4 percent, 2.6 percent, and 2 percent, respectively. As expected, the projects that teams are working on this year and into the next include business intelligence, mobility, and cloud computing, at 49 percent, 48 percent, and 40 percent, respectively.[2]

Follow the Money

I strongly believe that the money that CIOs around the globe are currently investing or planning to invest in the near future indicates the technical areas that CIOs and IT leaders need to focus on and, more important, be knowledgeable in. In the first edition, I examined a Robert Half technology poll of approximately 1,400 CIOs and found that the following areas were the focus of their spending and investments:

- Network security (35 percent)
- Database upgrade and installation (16 percent)

Project Priorities
You're most likely to invest in these technology projects this year:

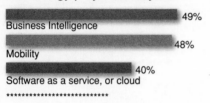

49% Business Intelligence

48% Mobility

40% Software as a service, or cloud

****

IT Spending by Company Size
Percentage of revenue

6% Small companies

4% Midst companies

3.7% Large companies

IT Spending by Industry

Industry	IT Budget as % of Revenue
High-tech/telecom/utilities	7.6%
Financial services	6.1%
Average of all industries	4.7%
Healthcare	4%
Manufacturing	2.6%
Retail/wholesale/distribution	2%

Exhibit 2.1   Your Spending

- Customer relationship management (CRM) systems (15 percent)
- Data storage and backup (13 percent)
- Wireless communications (10 percent)[3]

A *CIO* magazine survey of 231 respondents reported that the following four categories expected to increase in spending:

1. Security software
2. Storage systems
3. Computer hardware
4. Data networking equipment[4]

According to *CIO* magazine's "State of the CIO 2005" survey, the respondents indicated that the top technologies for innovation were re-designing IT architectures (73 percent), data access and warehousing (55 percent), and Web services (49 percent). From a global CIO priority perspective, CIOs in the United States, Japan, South Korea, Germany,

Australia, and Canada indicated that the top three technical priorities in 2005 were to integrate and enhance systems and processes, ensure data security and integrity, and focus on external customer service and relationship management.[5]

Fast-forward to today. Forrester Research in Cambridge, Massachusetts, identified the IT spending trends listed next in 2012–2013 for the United States and globally.[6]

United States

On a currency-adjusted basis, the U.S. market was projected to grow by 7.1 percent in 2012 and 7.4 percent in 2013.

- Computers and peripherals increase from $103 billion in 2012 to $112 billion in 2013.
- Communications equipment increases from $92 billion in 2012 to $94 billion in 2013.
- Software increases from $232 billion in 2012 to $259 billion in 2013.
- IT consulting services increases from $190 billion in 2012 to $207 billion in 2013.
- IT outsourcing increases from $195 billion in 2012 to $207 billion in 2013.
- Telecommunication services increases from $212 billion in 2012 to $231 billion in 2013.
- IT staff spending increases from $241 billion in 2012 to $258 billion in 2013.

The numbers underlying these totals show where the real action will take place and are thus focal points for CIOs:

- Mobile applications and middleware (up 14 percent): 54 percent surveyed.
- Business intelligence (up 14 percent): 46 percent surveyed.
- Security software (up 8 percent): 38 percent surveyed.
- Collaboration software (up 5 percent): 35 percent surveyed.
- Enterprise application stores (up 6 percent): 35 percent surveyed.
- Industry-specific applications (up 9 percent): 34 percent surveyed.
- Software as a service total (up 15 percent): 25 percent blended surveyed.
- Enterprise social networking tools (up 4 percent): 27 percent surveyed.
- Big data solutions (up 6 percent): 20 percent surveyed.

Globally

On a currency-adjusted basis, the global technology market was projected to grow by 5.4 percent in 2012 and accelerate to 8 percent in U.S. dollars in 2013.[7]

Outsource spending was projected to grow consistently in 2012 and 2013, at 6.7 percent and 6.0 percent, respectively. After a good run up in 2010, the demand for communications equipment (e.g., routers, switches, video conferencing, broadcasting, and two-way radios) was projected to slow to approximately 3 percent, then run up to 4.6 percent, in 2012 and 2013.[8]

- Computers and peripherals increase from $438 billion in 2012 to $477 billion in 2013.
- Communication equipment increases from $342 billion in 2012 to $358 billion in 2013.
- Software increases from $529 billion in 2012 to $583 billion in 2013.
- IT consulting services increases from $427 billion in 2012 to $465 billion in 2013.
- IT outsourcing increases from $385 billion in 2012 to $408 billion in 2013.

The research shows that while overall IT spending increases, the actual strength will be determined in 2013 and based largely on the economic environment in the European Union, China, and the United States. The fastest growing IT markets are in the following countries:

- Brazil (15.1 percent)
- India (14.3 percent)
- Mexico (14.3 percent)
- China (13 percent)
- Australia (8.2 percent)
- United States (6.6 to 7.1 percent)[9]

According to Forrester Research, "Asia, the Americas, and emerging markets partially offset [the] shrinking European IT spend," which is primarily due to the economic troubles in Europe. The forecast for IT growth in Europe as a whole is less than 2 percent. Italy and Spain are projected to have *negative* growth of 1.5 to 2 percent.[10]

According to the *Washington Post*, U.S. government spending on IT is projected to fall 0.75 percent, to $78.8 billion, in 2013. The U.S. government is one of the largest purchasers of goods and services worldwide, and just the Department of Homeland Security alone is expected to spend $729 million on IT in 2013. This is an increase of more than 20 percent from the cuts in 2012, because of cyber security research. Another $2.2 billion is expected to be spent in emerging technologies, $3 billion for education in science and technology, and $30.7 billion for appropriations in bioeconomy and medication research at the National Institutes of Health (NIH).[11]

Security and cloud computing are likely to be priorities for U.S. government spending in the near future. Since 2009, more than 35 agencies migrated to cloud computing environments, while another 30 or so are expected to make the leap in 2013.[12] Migrating to the cloud will probably result in the shutdown and reduction of government-owned and government-operated data centers and potentially a loss of IT jobs servicing those data centers.

Workforce computing, PCs, servers, systems management, data centers, disk storage, maintenance on existing technologies, and the like consumed approximately 23 percent of the total IT hardware budget in 2011, with a projected decrease in the next two years as a result of Windows 7 rollout completion and the adoption of bring your own device (BYOD) to work. Forrester believes that "security and efficiency" will "trump user choice and experience" as a result of planned IT professionals prioritizing their spending. The research advisory firm suggests the following priorities:

- Significantly upgrade security.
- Roll out client virtualization technologies. These are well adopted in the server space to date.
- Add touch-screen tablets to end-computing options.
- Embrace BYOD programs.
- Finish migrating to Windows 7 in advance of planning to deploy Windows 8.[13]

The Major Technology Trends Driving Change

As indicated in the previous section, it's easy to see that what companies are spending their money on provides a window into the trends that are driving innovation. In a recent report, Forrester Research identified the following five technology trends to watch:

1. **Cloud computing.** Web hosting, e-mail, and several mainstream enterprise resource planning (ERP) applications have made it into the cloud and are projected to expand in the coming years.
2. **Mobile applications and devices.** The consumerization of mobile devices has driven BYOD today. IT departments are leery to

provide support for personal devices that the company doesn't own, but security of the company's data is the concern today and in the future.

3. **Social media.** Facebook, YouTube, Twitter, and LinkedIn are highly trafficked sites today, with more and more companies trying to figure out how to use them to make money and service their customers. The return on investment (ROI) is tricky, though—the number of channels that companies are being forced to use because of consumer use just increases the costs.

4. **Business intelligence.** I've been writing about business intelligence for almost 10 years. The more channels, the more data, thus more of a need for analytics and business intelligence. It will help organizations make sense of their data. Big data, culled from web usage and social media channels combined with CRM, will continue to be a driver for increased investments in business intelligence.

5. **Virtualization.** The server market was the initial priority for virtualization. Now companies virtualize everything: storage, switches, firewalls, security appliances, networks, and client devices.[14]

① Cloud Computing

The following are some interesting statistics that support the adoption and innovative use of cloud computing:

- A billion monthly active users accessed Facebook's website at the end of September 2012, and 81 percent of them were outside the United States and Canada.[15]
- Twitter, a communications tool that's funded primarily by advertising, experienced an average of 340 million tweets per day.[16]
- The global private cloud market was $7.81 billion in 2011. It's predicted to reach $15.93 billion by 2015.[17]
- The software-as-a-service (SaaS) market represents the largest portion of the global cloud market, at $21.2 billion in total revenue in 2011.[18]

② Mobile Applications and Devices

Consumer markets are shaping the use and adoption of mobile computing in corporations, academic institutions, and organizations around the globe at a rapid rate. The following are some interesting statistics that support the adoption and innovative use of mobile devices and applications:

- Simple message service (SMS) is still the most widely used application in the world, primarily as a result of the low technology entry point (cell phone or simple computing device) across the existing cell tower wireless transmission channels. In 2011, there were 8 trillion SMS messages sent per day, an increase of more than a billion from the previous year.[19] That's 253,000 per second!
- About 29 billion smartphone applications were downloaded in 2011.[20]
- According to a new International Data Corporation (IDC) forecast, the market for mobile applications will continue to accelerate; the number of downloaded apps is expected to increase from 10.9 billion worldwide in 2010 to 76.9 billion in 2014.[21]
- Worldwide mobile apps revenues will experience similar growth, surpassing $35 billion in 2014.[22]
- YouTube received 25 percent of the traffic and 40 percent of the views from mobile devices in 2012.[23]
- Smartphone and tablet sales will surpass 1 billion in 2013.[24]
- Gartner Research predicted that 66 percent of mobile workers will own a smartphone in 2016.[25]

Social Media

Some recent findings released by Edison Research indicates the following trends in the use of social media:

- About 68 percent of Americans using social networks in 2011 indicated that none of the networks influenced their buying.
- In 2012, 47 percent indicated that Facebook had the greatest influence on purchasing behavior.
- Twitter users are 33 percent more likely to be Democrats.
- The fastest growing segment in social media is 45- to 54-year-olds.
- About 54 percent of Facebook users access the site via a mobile computing device, and 33 percent of the users access the site as their *primary* mechanism.[26]

Business Intelligence

Business intelligence (BI) tools and usage are evolving to focus on social media analytics. BI servers and data are moving to the cloud, and usage accessed by mobile devices (PDAs and tablets) is increasing every quarter. Consider the following:

- Twitter offers advertisers two layers of analytics that provide in-depth insights regarding paid and unpaid activity today.[27]

- BI tools are heading toward Web and cloud-based tools that are easier to use. A recent *Information Week* survey found that in organizations that used BI, only 25 percent of the employees had access to those tools, primarily because of the complexity of their use.[28]
- According to Gartner Research, operational and tactical BI is growing at a rate of 13 percent.[29]
- According to a 2011 survey of the BI Leadership Forum, more than 33 percent of organizations that use BI have purchased cloud-based BI. Of those organizations, 65 percent are planning to increase the use of cloud in the coming year.[30]
- Mobile BI is a trend of the future, and it's rapidly approaching. Gartner Research predicts that 33 percent of BI usage in 2013 will take place on a mobile device such as a PDA or tablet computer.[31]

⑤

Virtualization

Virtualization has matured in the data center, especially for servers, and is expanding for other network and security devices. Vendor dominance has come to two vendors: Microsoft and EMC/VMWare. Expansions for virtualization will take place on end-computing devices and compete directly with new end-computing operating systems. Consider the following:

- Gartner Research expected that 48 percent of all installed applications would be using EMC/VMWare virtualization software by the end of 2012.[32]
- About 58 million virtual machines were expected to be running by the end of 2012.[33]
- Virtualization has quickly moved beyond servers. Significant growth trends are predicted for the virtualization of switches, security appliances, storage with both cloud vendors, and customers who manage their own data centers.

Consumers are helping to shape the mobile and cloud markets. It's commonplace for businesses, staffs, students, researchers, retirees, and so on to leverage a mobile device and store more and more data in the cloud. The old days of losing the content on your smartphone or another mobile device are coming to an end. Devices like Apple's iPhone provide customers with an autosynchronization feature that automatically backs up their data to a secure cloud storage repository. According to Forrester Research, the mobile platform leaders by 2016 will be Apple, Google, and Microsoft, with a projected 91 percent share of the U.S. smartphone market and a 98 percent share of the tablet computing market. Private Wi-Fi hot spots are anticipated to grow to 648 million by 2015, while public Wi-Fi is anticipated to expand from 1.3 million to 5.8 million. Mobile applications will grow from a $6 billion industry in 2012 to $55.7 billion by 2015.[34]

These statistics and trends might not be seen in other industries—ever. Innovation in the technology market will continue to be a leader and drive company product innovation, significantly contribute to sales and profits, and shape the way that billions of people in the world communicate, collaborate, and buy goods and services.

A very cool article that I recently came across highlights an innovation that leverages technology from several of the technology trends mentioned earlier. According to CNN Money, the U.S. Food and Drug Administration (FDA) just approved the use of a "digital pill."[35] Patients ingest the digital pill whenever they take their medications, and it makes an electronic recording of the time that each medication was taken. This information is relayed through the skin to a patch worn on the body that in turn can send data to a mobile device, a tablet computer, or even the patient's physician or nurse, if authorized. The real-world practical applications for this type of innovation are amazing, especially as people age. It's common for a senior citizen to forget to take a medicine, which can be dangerous.

Another emerging trend that piggybacks on the transmission of personal data is the developing market for electronic personal data management via cloud technology. Forrester Research anticipates that this market is worth billions and could substantially increase in the coming few years.[36] Imagine the smartphone of the future, with none of the content stored locally on the device, but read and written on the cloud. If this type of marketplace takes hold, it could greatly alter the existing mobile device landscape and vendor market share leaders—including Apple, Google, and Microsoft.

An article published in the *Washington Post* notes that the University of Maryland at College Park, my undergraduate school, is innovating with mobile application technology. The article describes a new Maryland program dubbed Escort-M that is installed on a smartphone and allows students walking home late at night to be virtually connected to campus security as their online escort.[37] The system connects students with security professionals through an app, links to real-time cameras, and utilizes voice through the mobile device to improve public safety. This is very cool and definitely innovative. We are just scratching the surface with regard to what the future holds.

I asked my distinguished CIO and IT executive panel members their thoughts on the drivers that are affecting the role of the CIO and IT as an industry today. Their insightful answers are presented in the following CIO survey.

CIO SURVEY

What are the key drivers for the rapid change in the CIO role?

- I believe the availability of data, both transactional (e.g., credit card, banking, and buying habits) and attitudinal (e.g., preferences, social beliefs, political beliefs), combined with the ability to correlate these with things like weather and global economic trends, has allowed the CIO to take on the role of a true chief *information* officer. As the CEO of Intel Inc. once said, "There is no excuse for not knowing."

- I believe that the constant cyber threat continues to make the CIO and chief information security officer (CISO) roles more important than ever. Brand damage, loss of competitive information, and loss of money from cyber theft continue to be threats to a CIO.

- I also believe that changing world demographics—digital natives, emerging markets (South Korea, Brazil, and Turkey), and an aging U.S. population—have made the expectations for access to technology and information different from ever before. Simple user interfaces in multiple languages, accessed on mobile devices and with the ability to perform financial transactions and view data, are expected.

—*Ed Anderson, International CIO, World Vision International*

- As more business leaders become savvy in technology and hear the siren call of SaaS or consumerization offerings of IT products and services in the marketplace, IT leaders need to embrace these industry developments and lead the corporation in analyzing and adopting these offerings as they make sense. In essence, IT leaders need to work with their business partners and constituents as brokers rather than as order takers.

—*Joshua R. Jewett, SVP and CIO, Family Dollar Inc.*

- The focus on new technologies such as cloud computing and mobility are important. These are the business and technology strategies that are increasingly present in the IT field. Administrators and executives are under constant budgetary pressure, which pushes them to these new possibilities.

—*Denis Garon, Associate with the Secretary of the Chief Information Secretariat of the Council of Treasury*

- The key driver is the need for companies to change quickly in order to maintain a competitive advantage, increase productivity, and grow their business. Using information properly can help with that. What systems or networks are used is almost irrelevant anymore, given the enhancements in hardware, software, and communications (again, almost a commodity).

—*Earl Monsour, Director, Strategic Information Technologies, Maricopa Community College District*

I see the following drivers:

- The manner in which social media affect organizations' interactions with customers, understanding of customers (analytics), and internal work processes.
- The continuation of consumer-driven adoption of mobile technologies.
- The evolving use of technology as a service (e.g., SaaS, cloud computing services).

—*John Sullivan, CIO, American Chemical Association*

- IT has grown significantly in the last three to five years. With the consumerization of IT, CIOs have to consider that crucial data can easily flow in and out of an organization. It is far easier for internal users to use personal devices (e.g., phone or tablet) to access data. The challenge is to build the right mix on security and not hinder productivity.

—*Sanjay Khatnani, President, J2 Solutions*

What technology trends are most important to IT leaders today, and why?

- Cloud computing. It's a complete shift in how we deliver solutions, run technology, and manage vendor relationships and contracts. It's predicated on a service-oriented architecture (SOA) foundation and strong interoperability capabilities. The cloud also dictates federated risk management and mature SLA development.
- Mobile device neutrality. We can no longer assume the PC is the primary device for end-users. We need to develop open solutions that will work on any device (i.e., build this into the solution in version 1.0). It cannot be an afterthought.

(Continued)

CIO SURVEY   (*Continued*)

- Social media. Customers and employees are increasingly living a larger part of their lives virtually, in social media settings. This evolution will increasingly permeate corporate settings, and as IT leaders we must support and enable this trend through enterprise social media. Knowledge workers will expect all of the productivity associated with seamless online collaboration. Companies that do not embrace this trend will be at a competitive disadvantage and will have a hard time attracting talent.

- Semantic Web and solutions. Building additional intelligence in all things, Web as well as IT solutions, will lead to a more rapid delivery, an increased value, flexibility, and the sustainability and reuse of solutions. We are seeing this in the next generation of business process management system (BPMS) solutions and the table-, rules-, and role-driven workflow engines that understand the relationship of things in the solution.

—*Peter Classon, Partner, LiquidHub Inc.*

- Cloud computing and mobile technologies are most important because they let the CIO scale up operations more rapidly, as needed, and enable the business applications and data to be available from any device and any place in the world.

—*A. Murat Mendi, CIO, Ulkdar Holding*

I see many drivers. Three include:

- Use of consumer products
- Network expansion
- Virtualization

—*Ray Barnard, SVP and CIO, Fluor*

I see four clear drivers:

- Consumerization of IT
- Expansion of mobility
- Virtual desktop infrastructure (VDI)

- Cloud computing

—*Joel Schwalbe, CIO, CNL Financial Group*

- Cloud, SaaS, infrastructure as a service (IaaS), and business analytics are the trends I believe are transformational, because they move the CIO from the construction business (development of solutions) to the "What do I do with the freed-up resources, newly acquired information, and newfound technology choices?" business. I think CIOs need to continue to think of these new solutions as additional tools in their portfolios that allow them to shift resources from non–value added services (and commoditize them) to buying or renting them to focus on the services that transform their organizations.

—*Ed Anderson, International CIO, World Vision International*

Predictions for the Future

So, what do today's drivers of technology, regional and global spending trends, and a paradigm shift in the way we support computing (some of it on the financial books, some end-computing devices) and deliver solutions from disruptive to mature technologies? What will technology and the role of the CIO be in the future? Five years from now? How about in 2020? According to a *CIO* magazine article, top CIOs predict the future four years from now—2017. The IT executive role of the CIO will still be needed in the future.

The technology drivers of today—cloud computing, mobile computing, social media, and the consumerization of IT—aren't likely to change the role of the CIO tomorrow. What could be the CIO's ability to "handle and spark major business shifts" may also determine the effectiveness of the role. This is the belief of Steve Rubinow, the former CIO of the New York Stock Exchange and the current CIO of FX Alliance. "CIOs should always understand the pace of technology change. Now, it's just smaller and smaller time frames" to make the right decisions.[38]

The CIO of 2017 may be the following:

- An entrepreneur who can inspire staff and persuade suppliers to collaborate.
- A connector who links people across the company and facilitates collaboration.

- A global talent scout as recruiting moves beyond the bounds of the company's home country.
- A futurist who can predict trends and the implications of those trends.
- A master of business metrics. Innovation will become a criterion worth measuring.[39]

What will the role look like even later, such as in 2020? The following are several predictions:

- Microsoft's reign may end. Heterogeneous client computing will be driven by iOS and Android.
- The IT department won't be physical and may move into the cloud as well.
- Hyperkinetic business collaboration will occur in the cloud and across organizations, making security that much harder.
- CIOs will manage fewer humans, especially for security, as a result of advances in artificial intelligence.
- End-users will not be in departmental groups but will be replaced by Facebook-like virtual networks.
- Cyber warfare will turn the CIO into a general, as the interconnectedness of companies and suppliers increases.
- BYOD will be the norm. CIOs will adapt or get run over by users and staffs.
- Outsourcing will use artificial intelligence to enhance speech recognition and change the delivery of services like the help desk.
- CIOs will affect the business direction and be involved in business decisions, not just be told about them after the fact, as is often the case today.
- Analytics and business intelligence will be increasingly important and probably run from the cloud.[40]

What Did I Do to Prepare?

Preparing for the future is a bit like trying to look inside a crystal ball, see exactly where you'll be in your career years from now, and have a road map to get you there. Unfortunately, that's not the case. As a result, what I do to prepare for the future is to stay educated and abreast of the latest IT and business trends so that I'm not reacting to them but adapting to them. Specifically, what I've done is not so much to *prepare* as to *adapt* to the changes in IT as well as the role of the CIO:

- I developed a cloud strategy in my organization two years ago, integrated it into the IT strategic plan, and set our organization on a path to a new enterprise architecture that includes the components of public and private clouds. We've rolled out two large enterprise applications that leverage the cloud in the past 15 months. So far, so good.

- Adopting cloud computing changes everything, especially integration strategy. I essentially started from scratch, researching the latest technologies and enterprise business solutions that offer cloud-to-cloud, cloud-to-premise, and premise-to-premise secure integration solutions with the sample tool set. My team has implemented several integration orchestrations between cloud products and some of our internal systems. Doing so has allowed us to improve our integration approach through smarter technology, implement batch and near real-time data exchanges, and better support the business. There are some good options out there. Check out Cast Iron (IBM), Web-Methods (Software AG), Pervasive, and Boomi (Dell) cloud integration tools. Forrester and Gartner both have some great research on this topic.

- I adopted BYOD and have not looked back. It's here to stay and can actually help lower costs. I recently had a discussion in New York with a group of CISOs, and the topic of BYOD involved a large group of us. The CISO of a not-to-be-named top 10 financial services firm explained to me the elaborate legal and technical mechanism he went through to certify and support one device, the iPad. When I asked him whether the measures taken can totally protect the data on the personal devices, the answer, as I expected, was no. Given the plethora of backup mechanisms available to users for their personal devices, including automated cloud data synchronization, it's difficult to justify the cost and labor to lock them down. I recommend using data loss prevention (DLP) software to really know where your data is going.

- I'm rolling out a tablet pilot and engaging with vendors on VDI as I write this. If your workforce is mobile, you may have to wait just a little longer for offline virtualization on the client side, but it is coming.

Recommendations

My recommendations in this chapter are concise, because it's clearly harder to predict 10 years ahead. I look back and use trend extrapolation forecasting to remind myself of the tremendous rate of change that technology has gone through in the last two decades and, more important, the effects on society, individuals, and businesses. It's a bit humbling but still exciting to see what we've been part of. The following recommendations are intended to better prepare us all for the decade ahead:

- Leverage your existing and prospective customer base to learn about the business drivers and trends coming down the pike that will require IT innovation and services. Listening skills are just as important as technical skills.
- Make sure your network has the sufficient channels and links to individuals and groups who can educate and inform you. I find that vendors and cutting-edge companies who are innovating products and often creating new trends are the most informative. Just remember what our original reaction to MySpace was years back. Some thought it was a fad, others saw it a way to connect with friends, employers saw it as a distraction from work and a productivity hog, and advertisers saw it as the holy grail. Fast-forward to today—social media and networking are now integrated into the global society and affecting IT organizations around the world. Read the right journals and newspapers to stay abreast of the innovators in the world. I personally like the *Wall Street Journal*, the *Harvard Review, Entrepreneur, Inc.* magazine, Bloomberg business news online, *Science* magazine, and CNN.com.
- Keep up with IT advisory research firms and their reports and trends. I recommend Forrester, IDC, and Gartner.
- In addition to reading the fee-based research, keep current with the latest tools, product reviews, and blogs. My favorite online sites are eWeek.com, ComputerWorld.com, and CIO.com.
- Attend IT and business conferences and events. Network with vendors, customers, and companies to see what's in their pipelines. These events are great places to network for other purposes as well.
- Continue to feed your brain, and if you have the time and persistence, enroll in a certification program or advanced degree program that will augment your current experience and knowledge.
- Get engaged and drive cloud computing, institute social media initiatives (BI is a great one that can add value and help drive revenue for for-profit firms), pilot desktop virtualization, and launch tablet projects with mobile applications that integrate to your core applications and assist the mobile users.
- Adopt BYOD or die trying. I personally held out for as long as I could in my organization but recently succumbed to continuing end-user pressure and changed the IT policies supporting personal devices. According to the trends, research, and predictions for the future, it's here to stay, but it does come with risks that I'll further discuss in Chapter 8. Nothing is free.

- Don't ignore VDI. In addition to faster distribution of applications and potentially lower costs, it promises to improve the security of personal devices, including BYOD.

Notes

1. Eleanor Roosevelt, Inspirational Quotes, www.inspirational-quotes.info/dreams.html (accessed July 28, 2012).
2. "State of the CIO 2012," *CIO*, January 2012, 36.
3. "Safety First," Robert Half Technology press release, February 25, 2005, www.roberthalf technology.com/PressRoom (accessed February 27, 2005).
4. "IT Spending Projections Rebound Slightly in February," *CIO*, March 1, 2005.
5. Elana Varon and Lorraine Cosgrove Ware, "The State of the CIO around the World," *CIO* May 1, 2005.
6. Andrew Bartels, "US Tech Market Outlook for 2012 to 2013," Forrester Research, April 4, 2012.
7. Andrew Bartels, "Global Tech Market Outlook for 2012 and 2013," Forrester Research, January 6, 2012.
8. Ibid.
9. Ibid.
10. Ibid.
11. "Government IT Spending Key to Job Growth?" *Washington Post*, May 20, 2012, H1.
12. Ibid.
13. David K. Johnson, "Determine Your Workforce Computing Hardware Budgets for 2012," Forrester Research, February 23, 2012.
14. Ibid.
15. Facebook, Key Facts, newsroom.fb.com/content/default.aspx?newsAreaId=22 (accessed October 15, 2012).
16. Twitter, blog.twitter.com/2012/03/twitter-turns-six.html (accessed October 15, 2012).
17. Bartels, "Global Tech Market Outlook for 2012 and 2013."
18. Ibid.
19. "SMS Growth in Decline But Still Crushes Mobile Messaging Apps," Pingdom, November 8, 2011, royal.pingdom.com/2011/11/08/sms-growth-in-decline-but-still-crushes-mobile-messaging-apps (accessed November 11, 2012).
20. "29 Billion Smartphone Apps Are Downloaded in 2011," Digital Lifescapes, November 3, 2011, blog.geoactivegroup.com/2011/11/29-billion-smartphone-apps-are.html (accessed November 11, 2012).
21. "IDC Forecasts Worldwide Mobile Applications Revenues to Experience More Than 60% Compound Annual Growth Through 2014," International Data Corporation press release, December 13, 2012, www.idc.com/about/viewpressrelease.jsp?containerId=prUS22617910&sectionId=null&elementId=null&pageType=SYNOPSIS (accessed November 11, 2012).
22. Ibid.
23. Matt Swider, "Google Now Considers Itself a 'Mobile First' Company as YouTube Soars," TechRadar, November 10, 2012, www.techradar.com/news/internet/web/google-now-considers-itself-a-mobile-first-company-as-youtube-soars-1111545 (accessed November 11, 2012).
24. "Cynthia Harvey, "Gartner: Smartphone and Tablet Sales Will Top 1 Billion in 2013," Datamation, November 7, 2012, www.datamation.com/news/gartner-smartphone-and-tablet-sales-will-top-1-billion-in-2013.html (accessed November 11, 2012).

25. Ibid.
26. Tom Webster, "Why Twitter Is Bigger Than You Think," Edison Research, April 23, 2012, brandsavant.com/why-twitter-is-bigger-than-you-think/ (accessed August 23, 2012).
27. "Advertiser Analytics," Twitter, https://business.twitter.com/en/advertise/analytics (accessed August 3, 2012).
28. Jonathan Taylor, "Business Intelligence Trends for 2012," Klipfolio, www.klipfolio.com/resources/business-intelligence-trends-2012 (accessed August 3, 2012).
29. Ibid.
30. Ibid.
31. Ibid.
32. "Virtualization Market Statistics and Predictions by Gartner," Wordpress, eginnovations .wordpress.com/2010/06/18/virtualization-market-statistics-and-predictions-by-gartner (accessed August 3, 2012).
33. Ibid.
34. Ted Schadler and John C. McCarthy, "Mobile Is the New Face of Engagement," Forrester Research, February 2012.
35. Erin Kim, "Digital Pill with Chip Inside Gets FDA Green Light," CNN Money, August 3, 2012, money.cnn.com/2012/08/03/technology/startups/ingestible-sensor-proteus/index .htm? (accessed August 3, 2012).
36. Francesca Robin, "The Emerging Market That Could Kill the iPhone," CNN Money, August 1, 2012, tech.fortune.cnn.com/2012/08/01/iphone/?iid=obnetwork (accessed August 3, 2012).
37. Matt Zapotosky, "At U-MD., Safer Walks Home via Cellphone," *Washington Post*, May 28, 2012, B1.
38. Kim S. Nash, "Top CIOs Predict the Five-Year Future of the CIO," *CIO*, May 1, 2012, www .cio.com/article/print/704050 (accessed July 20, 2012).
39. Ibid.
40. John Brandon, "10 Predictions for What the CIO Role Will Look Like in 2020," *CIO*, May 3, 2012, www.cio.com/article/print/705599 (accessed July 20, 2012).

CHAPTER 3

IT Standards and Governance and the Impact of Consumer Devices

> Nothing can stop the man with the right mental attitude from achieving his goal; nothing on earth can help the man with the wrong mental attitude.
>
> —THOMAS JEFFERSON[1]

In the first edition, I talked about the importance of IT governance as well as the style and domains I've leveraged for the past 15 years of my career. The IT Governance Institute (ITGI) states that IT governance is "the responsibility of the board of directors and executive management."[2] Some organizations include the CIO in executive management, while others do not. I believe that IT governance is a responsibility of the board as a byproduct of risk management and that it is directly the CIO's responsibility to define and implement an institution's IT governance framework.

IT Governance and Its Benefits

ITGI defines governance as "the leadership and organizational structures and processes that ensure that the organization's IT sustains and extends the organization's strategies and objectives."[3] Two IT governance experts, Peter Weill and Jeanne Ross, defined IT governance more simply as "the decision rights and accountability framework for encouraging desirable behavior in the use of IT."[4] They described the following five key areas in the framework:

1. IT principles
2. IT architecture
3. IT infrastructure for shared IT services
4. Business application requirements for each project
5. IT investment and prioritization[5]

The benefits of governance include the following:

- Better alignment of IT with the business
- Delivery of technical solutions that meet business objectives
- Control of costs
- Management and monitoring of the IT portfolio, including joint business and IT projects
- Maximization of IT and business resources
- Compliance with audits and regulations
- Management and mitigation of risk

As a reminder from the first edition, Exhibit 3.1 shows a sample IT governance framework. It includes seven core domains that have helped me run a cost-effective and productive IT department for more than a decade. For specifics on the domains and interactions with constituents (e.g., vendors, IT staff, and business), please consult the first edition.

Governance Style: **Duopoly + IT Monarchy**
- Multi-domain with a focus on communication

Business Customers   **Management Committee**

Understanding Business Requirements and Delivering Value

Prioritization, Approval of Projects and Strategies

Relationship Building, Project Strategies and Communication

Coordination and Business Unit Ownership

Steering Committees, Business Unit VPs

CIO
IT Governance Plan
Domains:
- IT Principles, Policies & Procedures
- IT Architecture, H/W, S/W Standards
- IT Methodologies & Templates
- Project Plan Structure & Templates
- Change Management
- IT Strategies, Investment, Budgeting
- IT Audit and Compliance

Project Managers

Obey Governance and Communicate as Needed

Communicating / Enforcing Policies and Standards

IT Department   **Third-Party Partners Cloud Vendors**

Exhibit 3.1   Sample IT Governance Framework and Domains

How IT Trends Affect IT Governance

IT governance is a fairly common practice in the industry today, and it is as important as ever in guiding a changing IT environment and business trending landscape. In the past, it was fairly common for CIOs to use more rigid standards and homogeneous computing environments as a mechanism to lower costs (operating and labor), decrease technology complexity (through standards), and reduce risks. Today CIOs are being challenged by the consumerization of IT and by disruptive technologies that are affecting *how* IT is managed, including the effects on the IT strategic plan. The following trends are impacting IT governance and, as a result, altering the framework so that IT leaders can adjust and succeed:

- Cloud computing
- Mobile applications and devices, including bring your own device (BYOD)
- Social media
- Changes in business intelligence approaches and technology, most recently the shift to the cloud
- Virtualization

The effects of these trends on IT governance are occurring every day and are resulting in adjustments to frameworks, standards, processes, and strategic planning.

Cloud Computing

Cloud computing affects IT governance in several ways. It affects IT standards, resulting in a more heterogeneous computing environment. For example, CIOs who previously wanted to standardize on one or two database management systems are losing the battle and ending up with an environment that is now partly out of their control. As a result of losing control of the underlying technology components behind SaaS or cloud products, the environment can become more complex or, at the very least, shift responsibilities to entities outside the core IT department. Service level agreements (SLAs) become much more important. I'll discuss those in Chapter 4.

The cloud is no longer a myth in which only a few companies are taking the leap. Salesforce.com today boasts more than 104,000 customers, 16,000 in the nonprofit community alone—all in the cloud, with no software installations required by IT departments.[6] Salesforce.com is a perfect example of a successful cloud vendor that has a terrific CRM product in addition to some cool collaboration tools.

Now, back to the effects on standards and integration. The complexity and underlying components of the Salesforce.com database are not exposed, which changes the way IT organizations must interact with it and integrate. As a result, the number of databases and types is increasing, as is the core underlying technology to integrate cloud vendors with other cloud vendors and on-premise solutions. Ten years ago, it was common for an organization to have its CRM, financials, and human resource solutions under the control of an internally managed data center. A common technique used to control costs and training was to standardize on the database (i.e., Oracle or Microsoft) and integrate via smarter interfaces (e.g., database snapshots, ETL, or SQL) behind the firewall.

As a result of moving applications into the cloud, hiding the type and complexity of the database, standards expand and integration changes overnight. My organization recently implemented two large ERP systems—a financial system in a managed private cloud and a CRM system—through Salesforce.com's public cloud offering. As a result of needing to integrate these two applications with each other as well as with other applications behind the firewall, we rethought our integration approach and changed it completely. We selected an enterprise business solution from a tier 1 middleware vendor that allows us to securely integrate cloud-to-cloud, cloud-to-premise, and premise-to-premise using the same tool. We also chose to leverage server virtualization to improve fault tolerance and scale and to lend directly toward our disaster recovery and business continuity program. Today, I'm pleased with the newly architected and expanded standards we've adopted. They are performing as expected.

In addition to enhancing IT standards, integration, and security changes, cloud computing increases the reliance on a vendor's products, hosting, performance, and system uptime even more. As a result, SLAs become much more important. Some cloud vendors allow more flexibility than others regarding performance metrics, SLAs, and penalties. I've found that the larger the vendor you're dealing with, the less flexibility CIOs have with SLAs. For instance, it's common for organizations that have selected cloud-based solutions to settle for their base system uptime performance metric. When negotiating with many cloud vendors, CIOs lose some of the negotiation battles—frequently system uptime, as a result of a prebuilt and single version of an available solution. We recently opted for a 98 percent system uptime clause after tying to negotiate a higher percentage to no avail.

As a result, CIOs are sometimes at the mercy of a large vendor's contract. This type of limitation has happened to me personally throughout the years—recently with a CRM purchase and previously implementing a Bloomberg financial analytics system. At that time, I was heading up IT for the corporate finance division of a large financial services firm. We proposed several changes to the contract's base language only to receive a response that client modifications of the terms were not allowed. It was a "take it or leave it" agreement. Since there wasn't a viable competitor to Bloomberg back then, we took it.

CIOs also need to determine their data comfort and risk in the cloud. Traditional cloud solutions share as much of the solution as possible, including data networks, telecommunication circuits, security equipment, servers, disks, and even databases. Know exactly what is shared and what's going to be dedicated to your organization before you sign on the dotted line. If necessary, negotiate dedicated items that improve security and match the security-risk profile of your organization. Most solutions are customizable to some degree. That said, the more you dedicate, the more your monthly recurring cost (MRC) goes up. That's the game.

Mobile Applications and Devices

Advances in mobile computing, applications, and the trending adoption of BYOD to work is affecting IT governance as well.

First, the rapid change of mobile devices (e.g., PDAs and tablets) is radically altering IT standards and how IT organizations provide support. CIOs need to quickly decide how they want to play in this space. Should they manage the devices even though they are not the property of the organization and not technically on the books? Should IT departments cover the costs of the devices themselves and pay monthly service fees out of a central IT budget or charge the business units? Should IT departments provide support from the IT help desk for personal devices? These are all real-world questions that CIOs are dealing with every day. Unfortunately, there is no holy grail on personal devices and BYOD. CIOs are damned if they do (support, pay, or manage) and damned if they don't.

Second, the availability of mobile devices, their low entry costs, and the flexibility they provide the staff are introducing the concept of multiple devices per person and changing the approach for how applications are developed and deployed. It's common for an employee today to have three devices: a smartphone, a tablet, and a personal or laptop computer. Traditionally, IT standardized on the traditional computer, locking it down with imaging technology and managing it with group policies and software distribution technologies. The technology to manage tablets and phones is not necessarily be the same, and as a result, it may be more complex and costly for IT organizations to adopt—especially if they allow staff members to bring their own devices to work. On the smartphone market alone, there are hundreds of different devices and models as well as an array of carriers, operating systems, and security concerns that go along with each device. The market for managing multiple devices from different vendors is evolving, but it is not mature yet and, as a result, comes with risks and costs.

Third, the security risks associated with more devices from more vendors and with more carriers—especially the devices that are not owned by the company—introduce risks of viruses, data loss, and theft. Organizations that are security-risk averse simply block personal devices and stick with tried-and-true technologies that they can standardize on, manage, and control. Again, there is a variety of third-party and vendor security solutions available in the marketplace to assist CIOs and CISOs, but the market is nebulous, overlapping, and complex.

IT governance and risk management are often used in the same sentence. I believe that IT governance is intended to provide superior IT services at the best price and to reduce risk to a level that's tolerable for the organization. According to Forrester Research, "Risk is inherent in almost everything a business does or doesn't do." Forrester suggests that "good governance requires both a strategic and [an] operational approach to managing risk."[7]

So how does this affect mobile technology? Mobile technologies, as well as social media and cloud technologies, "have the potential to greatly enhance governance, risk and compliance (GRC) programs."[8] Examples of excellent use to aid governance are improved training through social media channels, incident response and notification through SMS, and enhanced security for staff through mobile applications and video technologies. I firmly believe that while mobile technologies are great and on the rise in use, they increase the risks for organizations in many ways.

Good organizations are making mobile device security a top priority in terms of risk mitigation and IT governance. The following are some noteworthy criteria for the mobile security landscape that can help CIOs and CISOs to better protect their institutions from risk:

- **Anti-malware.** Depending on the device operating system, anti-malware and antivirus technologies to mitigate risk vary in maturity. They can also be expensive and require multiple solutions, depending on the operating systems supported (iOS, Android, Windows Mobile). As a result, standardization can reduce the costs of both support and risk management.
- **Application control.** The ability to deploy and manage a plethora of mobile devices and operating systems often adds to the stress level of a security professional today. The more flexible an organization is with device "flavors" (vendors and operating systems), the more complex and costly it can be to manage the devices.
- **Authentication.** Operating system restrictions can make it hard for organizations to employ third-party authentication solutions. This

portion of the utility sector is also maturing, but it is not fully there because of the rapid growth of device type and the fragmentation of mobile operating systems.

- **Certificate management.** According to Forrester Research, "The ability to provision and manage application level digital certificates is a differentiating capability for mobile security products."[9]
- **Data loss prevention.** DLP vendor offerings have not fully caught up to the variations of mobile devices. Some vendors provide support for certain products but not others. As a result, DLP across the mobile layer isn't consistent and can't guarantee how secure sensitive company data may be.
- **Device compliance and network access control.** Network access control (NAC) might be employed to block data transactions and information from devices that are noncompliant with security software or applications that introduce more risks. NAC is mature for computers but not for mobile devices.
- **Device security and theft.** The smaller the device, the higher the probability of theft. Theft translates to corporate data risk. Organizations that employ BYOD but fail to wipe the asset clean after a reported theft may have additional risk.
- **Encryption.** Some mobile operating systems have built-in encryption for data at rest on the device, but others do not and require third-party software solutions. Again, standardization may reduce the risks here.
- **Network security.** This refers to the ability to implement a mobile virtual private network (VPN) to sensitive servers and applications combined with traditional perimeter protection, including firewalls and intrusion detection and prevention.
- **Privacy control.** Consumer noncorporate applications on personal devices that are connected to the organization's applications pit privacy concerns directly against organizational security and control. Some organizations I've spoken with don't allow BYOD because their lawyers believe that sound device management might infringe upon the individual's privacy, since the asset is not owned by the organization.
- **Selective wiping.** Selecting wiping refers to the ability to erase corporate installed applications and data while preserving the employee's personal data and consumer applications.
- **SMS and instant messaging archiving.** Organizations that are required to monitor and log business communications (e.g., e-mail, SMS, and instant messaging) push new complexities and costs associated with mobile devices, especially BYOD. Some mobile operating systems don't allow third-party applications to the device's SMS channel.

■ **URL and content filtering.** Organizations that monitor or block inappropriate content associated with the Internet for their workstations and computers now need to target mobile devices as well. Variations in operating systems' ability to integrate with third-party tools add complexity and costs.[10]

Social Media

Social media is still on the rise, even though many of the vendors who have gone public are having difficulty monetizing their user bases. I'll talk a lot more about social media strategies later in the book. At this stage, I'll limit the conversation to governance and risk. Anyone who has ever put in content filtering and social media logging technologies will tell you that these add the risk of sensitive corporate data leakage and can also greatly reduce staff productivity. In my previous role as the CIO of the World Wildlife Fund, the time staff spent on using personal social media sites was staggering. I can still recall my presentation and findings to the head of operations along with my recommendation to reduce access during business hours for non-business-related sites.

Social media is often the venue of choice for employees to gripe about coworkers and their employers in general. I do not recommend doing so, especially within organizations that monitor content. Just take a look at sites like www.glassdoor.com. I ran some newsworthy CEO names through its gauntlet and found that the openness and penchant for negative feedback was disturbing, in some cases. Also, several countries do not have the flexibility and freedom of speech that we have in the United States. Russia, Indonesia, Iran, and Turkey, for instance, don't take kindly to negative comments about government officials or leaders, and some of them have tremendous penalties, including jail.

In my search of several public social media sites, I often came across confidential material, including leaks about product launches and compensation. Several vendors now offer solutions to monitor and manage the risks associated with social media. Websense and Symantec are two of my favorites. Social media sites also pose risks for institutions in the form of phishing scams and malware. According to David Thompson, the group president and CIO of Symantec Services Group, "Social media is an opportunity for malware to come into an enterprise, as well as an opportunity for spear phishing attacks where a message is crafted to a specific agency or [an] individual is targeted to obtain certain information."[11] The explosion of social media use and the inclusion of categories in Internet content-filtering solutions are tools to mitigate risks.

That said, with the explosion of BYOD, managing social media sites and controlling risks can be tricky for today's security-minded CIOs. I'm still dumbfounded that some organizations do not monitor, block, and proactively protect their institutions from the risks associated with the Internet, including protecting confidential data and intellectual property from leaking out of the organization via mobile computing and social media. A recent *Washington Post* article revealed that the Pentagon's Missile Defense Agency "warned its employees and contractors recently to stop using their government computers to surf the Internet for pornographic sites."[12] Really? How about proactively blocking these sites and the risks associated with them in the first place? As a result, I'm a big fan of developing a comprehensive security strategy that is risk informed and that proactively takes steps and uses software to mitigate those risks.

Privacy concerns have been a risk issue long associated with social media. The *Washington Post* reported that the ghostwriter for Facebook's Mark Zuckerberg came to "unfriend the social media scene," recently swore off social media, and has gone off the grid.[13] Katherine Losse was Facebook's fifty-first employee, but she "became skeptical of the nature of relationships formed through social media, left the company, and ended up in the small West Texas town of Marfa." Her new book is titled *The Boy Kings: A Journey into the Heart of the Social Network*. The *Post* article describes how her thoughts "soured on the revolution in human relations she witnessed from within" Facebook and that "the explosion of social media left hundreds of millions of users with connections that were more plentiful but also narrower and less satisfying, with intimacy losing out to efficiency."[14]

The bottom line is this: Social media, privacy considerations, and personal use through corporate and computer networks add risks to an organization and begs to be addressed by the CISO and the CIO.

On the positive side, social media usage by individuals and companies is exploding. The future interaction with customers will be done through social media channels, most likely delivered to mobile devices, smartphones, and tablets. Some of the more progressive companies today are leveraging social media to better understand their customers and their competitors, to drive revenue through the applications available on social sites, and to serve their customers through the channels that the customers use and want to interact on—mainly Facebook and Twitter, via a mobile device. I'll have much more to say later about the absolute pros of having a great social media strategy within your company. The future is social, mobile, and through the cloud.

Business Intelligence's Shift to the Cloud

Business intelligence (BI) is also moving to the cloud, albeit not as fast as other technology services such as applications in the cloud (SaaS), Web hosting, collaboration, messaging, and e-mail. As the trend of the cloud progresses, traditional in-house BI installations will move into the cloud, where provisioning, patching, and performance management become commodity services for IT so that their teams can focus on the true benefits of BI solutions: mining data to expand an organization and better serve its customers.

BI in the cloud is just an extension of the effects of cloud computing on IT governance, plus a bit more. Moving to the cloud changes integration approaches from traditional extraction, translation, and load (ETL) to enterprise business–oriented solutions potentially *combined* with ETL. The real impact on IT governance is the security of the information contained within BI solutions. Simply put, moving BI into the cloud means that you are trusting another organization with the rich data within your BI system, which most likely includes customers, prospects, personal customer data, buying patterns, and Web click-stream data for those with significant Web presences. Decentralizing BI requires an additional focus on SLAs, background checks, and the security of the data at rest and in motion between enterprise systems. As a result, moving BI into the cloud requires more due diligence on the underlying contracts for the vendors who will hold your valuable data. As stated previously, your cloud strategy, including BI, should be carefully orchestrated and evaluated against a well-defined risk-based approach.

Virtualization

Virtualization is a technology that keeps on giving and maturing. It has allowed IT departments to completely change the way that servers and systems are provisioned and designed for fault tolerance and performance management. Some of the benefits are a much better utilization of processing capacity (i.e., a higher utilization of the central processing unit), faster provisioning and deployment, and greatly improved multisite disaster recovery capabilities.

The virtualization market is mature for servers and disk systems. It's evolving to include other components of the data center, including switches, firewalls, and intrusion and detection devices. As a result, it has changed the way CIOs manage their underlying core technologies and has directly affected IT standards, which is a component or domain of IT governance (as illustrated in Exhibit 3.1).

The next phase of maturity will come in the area of virtual desktop infrastructure (VDI), including the virtualization of operating system environments as well as individual applications. Vendor and product maturity are not the same in the VDI world as in server and data center virtualization. A current weakness is the ability to effectively deploy, run, and maintain a virtual desktop that's disconnected from the network. I'm referring to the road warrior who's often out of the office and sometimes out of connectivity to the corporate secure local area network (LAN) and application infrastructure. I predict that we're only 12 to 18 months away from some significant breakthroughs on this front. The current vendors leading the VDI charge are Microsoft, EMC/VMware, and Citrix. EMC/VMWare holds the lion's share of the server virtualization market.

Organizations that jump too soon to a leading/bleeding VDI vendor may experience vendor fragmentation and what goes along with it, including different products, code, integration and expanded vendor management, contracts, and legal documents. I encourage CIOs to develop a virtualization strategy that's based on business drivers and not IT drivers. Simply jumping into VDI without conducting financial and business due diligence is ill-advised and may cause more hassles than intended.

I asked my distinguished IT leaders several questions about the importance and benefits of IT governance and which models they employ. Their answers are included in the following CIO survey.

CIO SURVEY

How important are IT standards and governance models to you as a CIO?

- I would say high for both.

- As more standards are developed and accepted, it makes everything from hiring to choosing technologies easier. For example, I would hire a person who knows and follows the standards I have already established as policy in my organization.

- Governance models help to keep business and technology aligned. No investments should be made in technology unless the business and technology managers agree that there will be a return to the business as a result of the new technology.

—*Jay Seagren, Sr. Manager, Enterprise Systems, Pew Charitable Trusts*

- Moderately important.

- In my opinion, governance models are becoming increasingly less important and are used more to define a framework for change. At CNL, we've embraced a people-centric approach—so we're building to change versus building to last. Our emphasis on standards now focuses on protecting the confidentiality and sensitivity of CNL's proprietary and corporate information in an increasingly "always on, always accessible from anywhere" type of environment. To that end, we make every effort to support access from any location on any type of device—as long as we can protect and secure the content.

—*Joel Schwalbe, CIO, CNL Financial Group*

(Continued)

CIO SURVEY (*Continued*)

- Very important.

- Standards, in a decentralized federated model in a university, are absolutely essential to dealing with risk and also governance to get rapid decisions and proper authorization.

—*David Swartz, CIO, American University*

What are the top three benefits of implementing IT standards for hardware, software, databases, and architectures?

- Employee empowerment

- Risk mitigation

- Cost control

—*Joshua R. Jewett, SVP and CIO, Family Dollar Inc.*

- Regulatory compliance

- Consistency for staff and clarity for IT staff and end users

- Ease of integration and compatibility with other systems and new projects

—*Earl Monsour, Director, Strategic Information Technologies, Maricopa Community College District*

- It gives people something to ignore.

- It can save time and costs with integration and support activities. It saves money on licensing. It allows decision making to be delegated within specified parameters.

- It improves security and reduces the number of vendor solutions that need to be integrated.

—*John Sullivan, CIO, American Chemical Association*

What IT governance style(s) or model(s) do you use and why (examples: IT monarchy, federal, feudal, duopoly, none)?

- We are implementing a federal governance model in which the C-levels are the IT investment committee, and they review, approve, and prioritize each IT investment. We are just beginning this process, and so far, so good.

—*Ed Anderson, International CIO, World Vision International*

- I would describe our governance as primarily federal, in which large decisions and priorities are set by members of the senior leadership team.

- For IT-centric (security and infrastructure) decisions, we are more of a monarchy, with the decisions emanating from the IT leadership and little input from our business colleagues.

—*John Sullivan, CIO, American Chemical Association*

- We use IT monarchy in our company. The main reason behind this is the indifference of C-level executives in IT decision making. They see this as the sole responsibility of the IT management and team and hence usually approve the budget and projects that we bring in.

- My formal business education also helps create trust in them (C-level) to make the right decisions.

—*A. Murat Mendi, CIO, Ulkar Holding*

Portfolio Management of IT

Portfolio project management (PPM) is an important role for CIOs to embrace, regardless of whether they have a formal project management office (PMO). PPM of IT-related projects in an organization today is critical, and almost a necessity, to properly plan, evaluate, prioritize, monitor, manage, and track projects. The typical decision to start a PMO is often made as a result of things slipping through the cracks, which causes multiple project overruns, cost increases, or the implementation of projects that don't properly align with the business needs of an organization.

For IT organizations that don't use PPM and are having problems with project evaluation, approval, and implementation, PPM can help them gain control and will add a valuable component to an IT governance model. Organizations that have enough projects in the pipeline, that are trying to manage IT investments tied to business goals and objectives, and that are not consistently meeting their customers' expectations should consider PPM. A well-running PPM process, combined with other elements of the IT governance plan such as methodologies and IT standards, can provide the following benefits:

- Maximizing IT investments while minimizing risk.
- Improving communication between IT professionals and business and process leaders, thus opening the door to better IT alignment and more frequent communication with business leaders.
- Allowing the staff to better plan for resource allocation and to identify areas where resource and skill constraints may affect a project before it's too late.
- Reducing the number of projects to eliminate redundancy.
- Making it easier to stop a project that is not properly aligned or performing well.[15]

Regardless of the approach or software used, there is no one-size-fits-all solution to PPM. There are, however, plenty of resources and guidelines for implementing a best-practice PPM and PMO. A *CIO* magazine article provided the following key steps in establishing and managing IT projects:

- Perform an inventory of IT and business unit–related projects.
- Set up a process to evaluate candidate projects to ensure that they fit with a strategic objective.
- Create a fair process that includes business unit involvement to prioritize approved projects.
- Actively manage and review project status.[16]

According to Forrester Research, "Successful transformation strategies (information technology to business technology) will require a strong governance framework and a CIO capable of informing the decision making in the role of *portfolio strategist*."[17] Disruptive technologies like cloud computing, mobile platforms and devices, and virtualization (including VDI) has lowered the costs of providing IT-enabled business solutions as a result of these new emerging technologies. Doing IT portfolio management right includes paying attention to the collection of projects and investments through the oversight and management of current and proposed initiatives that involve IT capital and operating expenses. Forrester Research provides the advice shown in Exhibit 3.2 on building an IT portfolio management function with the right resources and responsibilities.

I encourage aspiring and sitting CIOs to invest in project portfolio techniques and software to run their departments as portfolios of business and IT investments and project candidates. I maintain a current list of projects in the IT

Area	Role	Responsibilities
Office of the CIO	IT oversight Holistic planning Governance	Strategic planning IT/business alignment Business results–oriented reporting
IT Financial Management	Financial oversight Financial acumen/savvy	Asset allocation Financial tracking chargebacks (if required)
Project Management Office (PMO)	Project tracking Project portfolio management	IT/business liaison Project tracking Project financial management
IT and Business Steering Committees	Review the "customer" portfolio	IT/business alignment Business/market alignment*

* *Chip Gliedman, "Building an IT Portfolio Management Function," Forrester Research, July 9, 2010.*

Exhibit 3.2   Project Portfolio Management Roles

portfolio at all times and require IT leaders to maintain them with current data. At the start of each month, I receive a collective CIO report with input from each IT subunit that includes project scorecards depicting the health of each active project in four areas: scope, schedule, budget, staffing. Exhibit 3.3 depicts the information at the individual project level that is included in the monthly report.

Exhibit 3.3   Project Scorecard Template

In addition to providing valuable information about the IT portfolio, project scorecards are good tools in meetings and discussions with business customers. The project portfolio also accompanies several other performance metrics (e.g., SLAs and uptime) and technical metrics (e.g., infrastructure performance and telecommunications utilization). Recommendations for IT portfolio management software are offered later in this chapter.

The IT Strategic Plan

A key component of IT governance includes the IT strategic plan. I maintain a three-year IT strategic plan and update it accordingly each year after the annual budget is approved by the board of directors. I typically include the following sections in an IT strategic plan:

- Executive overview
- IT organizational structure, including roles and responsibilities
- Key stakeholders
- SWOT analysis (strengths, weaknesses, opportunities, threats)
- Three-year financial and performance trends, including several key metrics:
    - IT operating, spending to revenue (compared with industry averages by sector)
    - IT help desk staff ratio (staff count per help desk resource)
    - IT operating cost of adding a new employee (operating budget and staff count)
    - Percentage of projects completed on time and on budget per year in the portfolio
    - Number of changes implemented to production systems by system
    - Percentage of help desk tickets meeting resolution targets by severity
    - Annual IT audit findings
- IT governance framework, including key domains
- IT mission, specific goals, and supporting objectives
- IT recommended infrastructure improvements (linked to growth or institutional goals)—three years
- Business recommended projects (linked to institutional goals)—three years
- Implementation plan and timing
- Risks and compliance

According to Forrester Research, an effective IT strategic plan has the attributes shown in Exhibit 3.4.[18]

Relevant to stakeholders	✓
Efficient—covers just what is needed	✓
Traceble—from performance measures back to business needs and drivers	✓
Documents assumptions and rationale	✓
Fits IT governance (decision-making, oversight) model	✓
Broadly communicated	✓
Has a direct impact on group and individual objectives	✓
Creation and maintenance is a process, not a project	✓
Document is living—regular review and update	✓
'Tells a clear story'	✓
'Just ambitious enough'	✓

Exhibit 3.4   Attributes of Effective Strategic Plans
Source: Forrester Research, Inc.

Forrester goes on to suggest the following five key phases of a solid IT strategic plan (see Exhibit 3.5):

1. Define the plan's purpose.
2. Capture and evaluate business needs.
3. Assess IT's ability to meet defined needs.
4. Develop plans to close any gaps.
5. Define the plan and implement.[19]

Depending on the sector and status of an organization (for-profit, non-profit, or educational) and countries in which it operates, the CIO should also note any challenges associated with meeting legal compliance requirements. Some noteworthy examples are as follows:

- **Sarbanes-Oxley.** Requires executives to certify that the company's financial statements are accurate and also requires organizations to establish a set of internal controls over financial accounting.[20]
- **Health Insurance Portability and Accountability Act (HIPAA).** A U.S. law and set of standards designed to protect certain health information about individuals.[21]
- **Fair Labor Standards Act (FLSA).** U.S. standards for minimum pay, overtime pay, and child labor.[22]
- **Basel III.** A global regulatory standard on bank capital adequacy, stress testing, and market liquidity risk.[23]

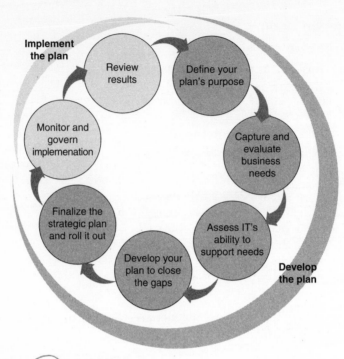

Exhibit 3.5 Phases of Strategic Plan Development and Ongoing Review
Source: Forrester Research, Inc.

What Did I Do to Prepare?

IT governance is an essential part of running IT to ensure that it's aligned to the business and that appropriate risks are mitigated in a manner fitting the culture of the organization. Regarding governance and the trends affecting IT today, I've taken the following path to prepare, and, more important, I've adjusted my governance framework and domains to be more flexible to adjust to changing trends:

- I regularly communicate and collaborate with other CIOs from a variety of industries to share information. From time to time I'll leverage a new or interesting technique I've learned into my three-year IT strategic plan. I maintain a three-year plan and update it regularly after the annual budgets are finalized and approved.
- To develop the cloud strategy, I held educational and briefing sessions with other executives and leaders in the organization. I've used the phrase

"CIO as the teacher to the C-suite" in previous discussions and articles on IT trends and governance. I truly believe that today's IT leaders are obligated to politely educate peers and superiors (including the board of directors) on the rationale for making changes to technology strategies, frameworks, governance models, and approaches—including technology opportunities like cloud computing, social media, virtualization, the consumerization of IT, and security. Today's CIOs *are* instructors to the C-suite for developing technical options and implementing change that is appropriate to the culture of the institution.

- I've adopted BYOD, albeit a bit against my will. After discussing this trend with many peers, I came to realize that the upside is greater than the downside, as long as CIOs who do adopt personal devices reengage and potentially redesign their information or device security approach. Mobile device management is key. DLP may be the right tool if your organization really wants to know where your data are going.

- I've researched social media technology trends, including social media campaigns and data analysis tools. There are some new cool tools in the market to conduct and analyze social media campaigns. I discuss specific tools in a later chapter. I'm working with our communications leader to understand her strategy and determine where I can add value. It will probably come in the form of IT advisory input and integration and data analysis. An additional note: BI tools and social media analysis tools are overlapping. I see some acquisition targets for the BI vendors in this space in the years to come—sooner than later, because I fully believe that BI tools are far more mature than purist social media analytics products currently on the market.

- I'm considering pushing BI into a private cloud. I'm not ready to leverage a public cloud for data that are most often used in BI tools to date. The primary reason for my hesitation is security.

- I'm continuing to virtualize as much as possible in our internal data centers. We're also preparing for a desktop virtualization pilot. VDI has evolved, but it isn't as mature as in the data center, primarily because of the business requirements for disconnected clients and devices. It will come sooner than later.

- I continue to maintain an IT governance framework that balances IT monarchy with IT duopoly. We use IT monarchy for pure-play infrastructure decisions and standards and duopoly for any business applications. I've added more weight to security, given the expansion into mobile computing, cloud computing, and social media.

- I've reengaged on security with a focus on data in motion. I believe that DLP shows the greatest promise as more organizations move to the cloud and adopt BYOD to their environment.

- I'm deploying mobile device management tools to better manage personal and devices on our books.
- I've refined the participants (IT and business) in our IT portfolio project process. Doing so exposes businesspeople to portfolio best practices and helps to build teams that can prioritize better. That's a key goal for me: to obtain a clear prioritization of projects and initiatives across the portfolio. I've also deployed a common project dashboard template for approved projects. Our project managers use it in meetings with customers.
- The IT strategic plan now has the components and considerations for making decisions on where a business or foundation technology component resides: inside our data centers (on-premise), in a private cloud, or in a public cloud. I've also expanded the metrics tracked on a monthly and annual basis within the framework of the IT strategic plan.
- I stay current on technology trends and products. I'm a regular user of IT advisory services to ensure that I'm looking at sound research in addition to marketing collateral about new products. I also network with CIO peers and select vendors to get different perspectives on how other organizations are deploying new solutions, changing their governance to adjust, and discussing options with C-level peers.

Recommendations

My recommendations in this chapter are concise, since it's clearly harder to predict three years ahead. I look back and use trend extrapolation forecasting to remind myself of the tremendous rate of change that technology has undergone in the last two decades and, more important, the effects of this on society, individuals, and businesses. It's a bit humbling but still exciting to see what we've been part of. The following recommendations are intended to better prepare us all for the years ahead:

- Research mobile device security vendors and their products, including AirWatch, BoxTone, Cisco, Good Technology, Juniper, Kapersky, McAfee, Maas360, Zenprise, and Mobile Active Defense.
- Check out IT portfolio management solutions from Oracle/Primavera and Microsoft. Cloud-based solutions are becoming more viable every day. Notables are found at www.innotas.com and www.powersteering software.com.
- Develop your project scorecard layout and information and include it in the monthly CIO report. Share this as appropriate with your

customers and keep your team members apprised of tasks, milestones, risks, and accomplishments throughout the project life cycle.

- Leverage your existing and prospective customer base to learn about the business drivers and trends coming down the pike that will require IT innovation and services. Listening skills are just as important as technical skills.
- Make sure your network has the sufficient channels and links to individuals and groups who can educate and inform you. I find that vendors and cutting-edge companies who are innovating products and often creating new trends are the most informative. Read the right journals and newspapers to stay abreast of the innovators. I personally like CIO.com, the *Harvard Review*, CNN.com, *Information Week*, and ComputerWorld.com.
- Keep up with IT advisory research firms and their reports and trends. I recommend Forrester, IDC, and Gartner.
- Attend IT and business conferences and events. Network with vendors, customers, and companies to see what's in their pipelines. These events are great places to network as well.
- Continue to feed your brain, and if you have the time and persistence, enroll in a certification program or advanced degree program that will augment your current experience and knowledge.
- Get engaged and drive cloud computing, institute social media initiatives (BI is a great one that can add value and help drive revenue for for-profit firms), pilot desktop virtualization, and launch tablet projects with mobile applications that integrate to your core applications and assist the mobile users.
- Get up to speed on social media technology, specifically Twitter, Facebook, and Salesforce. There are new tools on the market now that assist with developing, deploying, and monitoring social media campaigns that in the coming years will change how organizations cull data from and interact with social media sites. Check out Salesforce .com's new Marketing Cloud service. It's pretty amazing.
- Ensure that your internal network is the right size to perform when you push applications into the cloud. This includes paying attention to networking, security, and telecommunication circuits.
- Increase security and research the latest technologies designed to mitigate the risks associated with cloud computing, social media, and mobile devices, especially personal ones allowed to connect to the enterprise. DLP may be just the trick.
- Negotiate what you want with your cloud vendors, including system uptime, penalties, and the sharing of components (e.g., networks, servers, disk, security appliances, and databases). Separate the items that

keep you up at night from shared resources and pay a little more for dedicated components to ensure better security for your organization.

- Adopt BYOD or die trying. I personally held out for as long as I could but recently succumbed to continuing end-user pressure and changed the IT policies supporting personal devices. According to the trends, research, and predictions for the future, it's here to stay. Adapt or die trying.

Notes

1. Thomas Jefferson, Inspirational Quotes, www.inspirational-quotes.info/success-quotes.html (accessed July 14, 2012).
2. "Board Briefing on IT Governance," IT Governance Institute.
3. Ibid.
4. Jeanne Ross and Peter Weill, "Recipe for Good Governance," *CIO*, June 15, 2004, 36–42.
5. Ibid.
6. Company Milestones, Salesforce, www.salesforce.com/company/milestones.
7. Craig Symons, "IT Governance and Risk," Forrester Research, June 14, 2010.
8. Chris McClean, "Governance, Risk, and Compliance Predictions: 2011 and Beyond," Forrester Research, December 6, 2010.
9. Chenxi Wang, "Market Overview: Mobile Security, Q4 2011," Forrester Research, October 11, 2011.
10. Ibid.
11. Cindy Waxer, "CIOs Struggle with Social Media Security Risks," Public CIO, February 11, 2011, www.govtech.com/pcio/CIOs-Social-Media-Security-Risks-021111.html (accessed August 21, 2012).
12. "Workers Asked to Stop Watching Porn," *Washington Post*, August 5, 2012, A3.
13. Craig Timberg, "A World Away from Facebook," *Washington Post*, August 5, 2012, G1, G5.
14. Ibid.
15. Todd Datz, "Portfolio Management—How to Do It Right," *CIO*, May 1, 2003,
16. Ibid.
17. Craig Symons, "The CIO as Portfolio Strategist," Forrester Research, May 12, 2011.
18. Alex Cullen and Marc Cecere, "The IT Strategic Plan Step-by-Step," Forrester Research, April 10, 2007.
19. Ibid.
20. David J. Lineman, "Security Rules to Live By: Compliance with Laws and Regulations," Tech Target, searchsecurity.techtarget.com/feature/Security-rules-to-live-by-Compliance-with-laws-and-regulations (accessed August 24, 2012).
21. "Health Information Privacy," U.S. Department of Health and Human Services, www.hhs.gov/ocr/privacy (accessed August 24, 2012).
22. "The Fair Labor Standards Act (FLSA)," U.S. Department of Labor, www.dol.gov/compliance/laws/comp-flsa.htm (accessed August 24, 2012).
23. "Basel II and Cyber Law Compliance," NAAVI.org, www.naavi.org/cl_editorial_05/edit_may_20_05_01.htm (accessed August 24, 2012).

CHAPTER 4

Service Level Agreements

A Key to Improved Customer Expectations and Better Contracts

The talent of success is nothing more than doing what you can do, well.

—HENRY W. LONGFELLOW[1]

Customer service has new weight and focus for sales, marketing, IT, and communications professionals in a cloud-based, mobile, and social world. More than ever, teams need to pair up or work closely together as they hand off one service component to another, depending on the business and technical complexity. CIOs today must adopt new strategies and technologies to service their customers (internal and external) in the age of "mocial" (mobile computing intersecting with social media), often done in the cloud. This chapter provides some insights and recommendations for today's IT and business professionals.

Service in the Age of the Customer

CIOs today need to work more proactively with their C-level peers in leading with customer service. This applies to external customers and internal customers, or business users and staff. Forrester Research has called 2010 and beyond the "age of the customer."[2] Its report "Competitive Strategy in the Age of the Customer" described the following eras:

- **The age of manufacturing (1900–1960).** Companies that owned a factory—like Ford, U.S. Steel, and RCA—owned the market.
- **The age of distribution (1960–1990).** Businesses started globalizing, and retail moved into the suburbs in developed countries.

61

- **The age of information (1990–2010).** Networked computers, the Internet, powerful search engines, e-commerce, enterprise class systems, and the information within these systems helped companies fine-tune their strategies for products and distribution.
- **The age of the customer (2010–).** Global supply chains, Internet cloud computing, and mobile technologies are available to most companies, thus leveling the playing field. The ones that will flourish are the ones that best understand their customers and provide what the customers looking for at a competitive price and speed of delivery.

Today's buyers have more power than ever. Buyers can quickly search for product and price comparisons on the Internet, including through mobile Web access, and sometimes even dictate a price. Customers are sharing experiences with both service and products online in a social manner, influencing the market and competition as never before. As a result, customer service is even more important today, because it can make or break product or brand loyalty, which is no longer led by price.

According to the "Competitive Strategy" report, customers who are armed with technology are too powerful, resulting in the loyalty of satisfied customers. The analysis suggests that "it's no longer sufficient to be customer-centric or customer-focused"; a business must become "customer-obsessed." The Forrester Research report highlights the following characteristics of a customer-obsessed company:

- **Nimble.** Speed is emphasized over strength. Management structures are altered to permit the rapid pursuit of customers in new markets and new channels.
- **Flexible.** Versatility is valued over lock-in. Proprietary technology, locked-in contracts, and frequent reward programs don't create loyalty, they create barriers to leaving. Obsessed companies focus instead on meeting customer needs.
- **Global.** Worldwide supplies, demands, and markets are embraced. Goldman Sachs predicts there will be 800 million new middle-class customers from countries like India, Brazil, Russia, and China. Limiting a business to the home country won't drive sustainable growth.
- **Smart.** Products or transactions are information-rich rather than dumb. New applications with updated information, delivered across technologies to include mobile, are what customers are demanding now.[3]

The report suggests strategic and budget imperatives for a customer-obsessed company (see Exhibit 4.1).

Budget priorities	Strategic Imperatives		Budgeting Changes	
	Do more of this:	Do less of this:	↑$	↓$
Real-time customer insights for products	Combine real-time monitoring and database insights; search for unarticulated needs	Slow survey-based research, untargeted email blasts	Social listening platforms, customer intelligence	Traditional research surveys
Customer experience and customer service	Fund a customer experience group that works across channels	Customer service staff goaled on call volume	Comprehensive customer experience, call center training	Single-channel customer experience programs
Intelligent sales channels	Focus on end users and repeat business; build a customer database	Cram channels to inflate sales	Rich customer databases	Channel sales
Interactive content and marketing	Create content that drives inbound traffic; build mobile apps to engage customers	Knee-jerk social apps and advertising blasts	Goal-driven social and mobile apps, site content	One-way advertising

Exhibit 4.1   Strategic and Budget Imperatives for Customer-Obsessed Companies
Source: Forrester Research, Inc.

Customer-obsessed CIOs need to combine real-time monitoring and database insights, create mobile applications to engage customers and drive them to revenue-generating channels, employ social platforms and sites to glean their customers' and competitors' insights, and offer superior customer service.[4]

Few CIOs actually "own" the customer, since it is common for marketing, sales, and dedicated customer service departments to lead the charge. According to a global CIO customer satisfaction online survey, IT is very low on the ownership of customer satisfaction, policy, metrics, and service, with less than 10 percent in three primary domains (see Exhibit 4.2).[5]

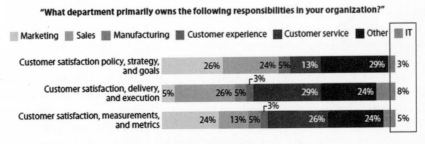

"What department primarily owns the following responsibilities in your organization?"

Base: 38 IT professionals

Source: Q3 2011 Global CIO Motivation And External Customer Satisfaction Online Survey

Exhibit 4.2   IT Is a Follower in Customer Satisfaction Planning, Delivery, and Metrics
Source: Forrester Research, Inc.

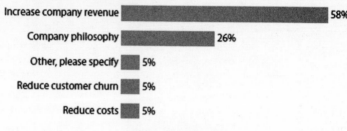

"What is your primary objective in increasing customer satisfaction?"

Increase company revenue	58%
Company philosophy	26%
Other, please specify	5%
Reduce customer churn	5%
Reduce costs	5%

Base: 38 IT professionals

Source: Q3 2011 Global CIO Motivation And External Customer Satisfaction Online Survey

Exhibit 4.3   Customer Satisfaction Is All about the Money
Source: Forrester Research, Inc.

When the survey respondents were asked what was the primary objective of customer service, their answers were not surprising (see Exhibit 4.3). Revenue was the highest priority, with 58 percent of respondents reporting, followed by company philosophy (26 percent), then dropping significantly to retaining customers (5 percent) and reducing costs (5 percent).[6]

Deciding whether to outsource customer service functions varies by company and industry; there is really no industry standard. Some organizations that can reduce costs by using offshore customer servicing firms do so after a deep analysis to ensure that they won't lose customers as a result of language difficulties between the supportee and the supporter.

I recently conducted an analysis on whether to outsource an IT help desk or keep it internal. Because of the high touch requirements for customer service and the culture of the organization, we were willing to have higher costs and less turnover of resources associated with an in-house solution, with more staff on-site, rather than a virtual solution. Some organizations don't have the luxury of paying a premium and, as a result, look for low-cost solutions. Because of the scope of discussing whether to outsource a customer service function, and the plethora of information available from fee-based IT advisory firms (like Forrester Research, IDC, and Gartner), I recommend researching and analyzing external information before taking the plunge and making a decision. The content and analysis alone could clearly fill up a book or two.

Customer service isn't just for existing customers; it's also for prospective customers. I recently reflected on just how important that is when I was evaluating two Web-based companies and the services they provide. I took Ancestry.com, an online genealogy service, and Zacks.com, an online investment research firm, for a spin to see if I wanted to become a formal customer on either one. Both have pretty cool services and provide interesting and helpful information. After test-driving both of these fee-based services, I decided to opt out, so I unsubscribed from both of the services through their process of doing so: one email-based, the other Web form–based. Both continued to send me e-mail advertisements long after I'd unsubscribed, even though I had received messages that I was in fact unsubscribed.

After becoming totally annoyed, I decided to contact their respective customer service departments to make it stop. After several e-mails and a request to speak with the head of customer service at Zacks.com, I finally got my name off that list. The amount of time I spent doing this surpassed the amount of time I spent trying out the service. Ancestry.com continued to send me spam and other unwanted mail for a month, even after I had spoken with a member of its customer service team. The response to me (September 9, 2012) was annoying and so memorable that I thought I'd share it with the readers:

> We apologize for any frustration this issue may have caused and appreciate your feedback. We have forwarded your message on to our Management Team for review. However, it can take up to 30 days to remove an email from our mailing list due to the cycle it is on.

In this day and age, I can't imagine a company servicing customers and prospects with technology and policies that take 30 days to remove an e-mail from a marketing list. Organizations today that are *really* focused on service in the age of the customer simply need to do better, or they will lose out to other companies that *are* paying attention to what customers and prospects want. Regardless of how cool I thought Ancestry.com's service was, because of the very annoying situation that this company put me through—including the time that it took to remedy my issue—I would *never* become a customer of Ancestry.com.

This example is just a subtle reminder to companies that the simple things really do matter and of what happens when trivial customer requests don't work well. Customer service will drive loyalty in the future as competition increases for products and services that customers can buy from a variety of organizations. Not doing customer service right has huge repercussions. In the future, companies will need to respond and meet customer expectations through a variety of channels, not just by e-mail and phone. The future of customer service is in social media. Those who do it well will grow.

Service Level Agreements

A service level agreement (SLA) is essentially a contractual or targeted level of service that a vendor or IT team is providing to its customers, internal and external. I offer the following definitions to help clarify:

- An SLA is a pseudo-contract or an actual contractual agreement between a service provider (e.g., IT staff or vendor) and the consumer or customer that outlines the service expectations for specific needs and the penalties for not meeting the contracted level.
- "An SLA is simply a document describing the level of service expected by a customer from a supplier, laying out the metrics by which the service is measured, and the remedies or penalties should the agreed upon levels not be achieved."[7]

In simplified terms, SLA components include the following:

- Specific elements of the services provided, including any conditions for services being suspended.
- Speed of response to issues raised, requests submitted, or tasks performed. This includes escalation processes and definitions. Common severity levels for services I've used are as follows:
    - **Severity 1:** Top-priority service request or a down production system or service.
    - **Severity 2:** High-priority service request, or the application or system is impeding the completion of a business process, with a large group or customer effect.
    - **Severity 3:** Moderate-priority service request, or the application or system is having a minor effect on the business, with a low number of individuals affected.
    - **Severity 4:** Low-priority service request or an enhancement to an application or a software or hardware purchase that's not time-sensitive.
- Speed and accuracy of the resolution of issues, requests, or tasks.
- Availability metric, measured in percentage, of a particular service offering or performance metrics for transactional work.
- Penalties for not meeting SLA goals or targets.
- Legal and managerial elements, including reporting frequency, measurement standards, dispute resolution, an indemnification clause that protects the customer from third-party litigation resulting from any breaches, and a mechanism to change or update the agreement.[8]

Most CIOs spell out SLAs for service requests and incidents logged to the IT help desk for their internal and external customers. Later in this chapter, you'll hear from my surveyed CIOs about how important SLAs are to them and where they draw the lines for key service targets and metrics. SLAs are also used heavily in contracts for IT services that are often performed outside the IT data center and within the reach of internal IT staff. Examples of contracts in which SLAs are important include the following:

- Hosting a public web site. Common system uptime targets include precision to four or five nines (i.e., 99.99 percent or 99.999 percent uptime).
- Hosting and servicing an e-commerce solution with an antifraud component.
- Hosting and servicing an enterprise-class software solution (e.g., Oracle Financials, SAP Manufacturing, Oracle/PeopleSoft Human Resources).
- Performing a customer service function (e.g., IT help desk for internal staff or external customers, customer call center, social media, smartphone).

It is a good idea to use SLAs because they do the following:

- Minimize risk, especially for contracted services.
- Set up-front expectations for customers, regardless of the channels through which they desire to be supported (social media sites, e-mail, web site, voice phone, smartphone, or SMS).
- Improve productivity for staff (internal SLAs).
- Contribute to customer loyalty and drive revenue (external SLAs).
- Establish clarity, roles, and responsibilities for all parties.

Cloud providers that offer massively redundant solutions can offer higher percentages for application or system uptime, some as high as 99.999 percent. It's common, however, to have a contractual targeted system or application uptime of 99.95 to 99.99 percent. Vendors who offer higher levels often also contractually require their customers to pay for redundant components at all levels to ensure that there isn't a single point of failure that could cause their site solution to fall below the targeted threshold.

The following examples provide some SLA terms from real contracts.

Contract 1: Large Global IT Hosting and Application Support Vendor

This contract includes the following services, SLAs, and penalties or credits. The measurement and calculation used to apply a penalty or credit is a weighted approach. For example, if the SLA that's not met is a system uptime service level, only 50 percent of the credit would apply.

Services

- Application or system hosting of 10 Oracle/PeopleSoft Financials system modules running on a redundant Unix environment.
- Application or support services (business and technical) in support of the system.
- Managed network and security services in support of the system.
- Managed backup and recovery services, including a multidata center site recovery plan.

SLAs

- Service request responses
  - **Severity 1:** 100 percent expected response within 15 minutes (25 percent of penalty-credit formula).
  - **Severity 2:** 90 percent expected response within 2 hours (20 percent of penalty-credit formula).
  - **Severity 3:** 80 percent expected response within 1 business day (5 percent of penalty-credit formula).
  - Mean time to repair a severity 1 service request: within 5 hours.
- System uptime (infrastructure and PeopleSoft application)
  - **Production system:** 99.5 percent (50% weight of penalty-credit formula).
  - **Nonproduction systems or environments:** 99.5 percent.
- Site recovery at the alternative data center within 24 hours, with the option of 12- or 24-hour-old data.

Penalties or Credits

- 10 percent of the monthly recurring costs (MRCs) if aggregate and weighted SLAs are not met within any given contract month.

Contract Termination Resulting from a Failed SLA

- The customer can terminate the agreement without having to pay a percentage of the remaining MRCs if the production system uptime target of 99.5 percent is not met for either 3 consecutive months or 5 months within a 12-consecutive-month period.

Contract 2: Small Regional IT Services and Help Desk Vendor

This contract includes the following services, SLAs, and penalties or credits. The measurement and calculation used to apply a penalty or credit is a weighted approach. For example, if the SLA that's not met is a system uptime service level, only 50 percent of the credit would apply.

The fixed monthly fees for this contract are based on the number of staff members supported, not the number of tickets submitted per month or an hourly rate for the resources providing support. This agreement also spells out the fees for increased or decreased numbers of staff members, which is very flexible to the customer and produces known costs regardless of the volume of support work performed.

Services

- Managed network support, including security and firewall services.
- LAN and cloud application account administration.
- Remote and on-site IT help desk or ticket services and support.
- Desktop support, including security end-point management.
- Asset management.
- Vendor liaison services, specifically to cloud-based e-mail, phone, and collaboration solutions
- Windows or server and networking patch management.
- Synchronization of PDAs and support for e-mail services.
- Content or URL filtering.
- Technical administration and support for on-site servers, networking, security, and network attached storage.

SLAs

- Service request responses
  - **Severity 1:** Response within 15 minutes, resolved within 4 hours.
  - **Severity 2:** Response within 1 hour, resolved within 4 hours if on the current business day, or 2 hours on the next business day if after business hours.
  - **Severity 3:** Response within 4 hours, resolved within 1 to 2 days.
  - **Severity 4:** Response within 1 day, resolved in 3 to 5 days.
- System uptime (infrastructure and PeopleSoft application)
  - **Production system:** none specified, since the architecture has redundant equipment across key layers (server, storage area network, Internet connections to cloud systems)

Penalties or Credits

- None

Contract Termination Resulting from Failed SLA

■ The customer may terminate the agreement without penalty at any time with sufficient notice if the service level is not meeting expectations. The customer is required to pay only the fees incurred to the separation date, not any remaining fees associated with the standard contract termination date.

SLA and Contract Differences

SLAs for standard IT help desk services differ from SLAs for traditional contracts for hosting or application services because the services performed vary. Exhibit 4.4 is an example of an IT help desk SLA using in-house IT staff.

This example distinguishes between standard help desk requests for end-user computing, account management, and device support, on the one hand, and support associated with a complex enterprise-class system like SAP, Oracle/PeopleSoft, or Salesforce.com, on the other hand. Following are some typical IT help desk customer issues:

■ Requesting a new PDA or smartphone.
■ Servicing a computer or laptop.
■ Requesting a computer loan.
■ Requesting a computer peripheral (ergonomic keyboard, mouse, headset, data key, CD-RW, or other supply).
■ Requesting a monitor upgrade.
■ Servicing a printer (e.g., error or toner).
■ Requesting a user account password reset.

	IT Help Desk Requests		Enterprise System Requests	
	Response	Resolution	Response	Resolution
Severity 1	15 minutes	4 hours	1 hour	4 hours
Severity 2	1 hour	8 hours	4 hours	8 hours (functional) 5 days (technical with change control)
Severity 3	8 hours	3 days	8 hours	3 days (functional) 7 days (technical with change control)
Severity 4	2 days – primarily to identify the right team to respond / form a team.	5 days	2 days	N/A (dependent upon resource availability, requirements, funding)

Exhibit 4.4   Company A: IT Help Desk and Enterprise-Class System SLAs

- Freeing a locked user account (most likely from entering multiple failed passwords).
- Requesting an e-mail distribution list to be created or for users to be added to an existing list.
- Requesting a software installation (e.g., Microsoft Project, SPSS, Adobe Acrobat Pro.)
- Sending a print job to an alternative network printer
- Reporting a virus.
- Reporting spam or inquiring how to add an e-mail address to a spam accept or block list.

These types of help desk requests, often called *tickets*, are different from the support requests associated with more complex and costly systems, such as the ones listed above from Oracle and Salesforce.com. Ticket requests for enterprise-class systems include the following:

- Asking how to do or process something (e.g., how to approve an invoice or create a purchase order).
- Requesting an application enhancement (e.g., adding a list of vendor names and contacts to a pull-down list when reviewing invoices for approval, creating custom routing for approvals based on invoice amount, etc.).
- Fixing incorrect data in the system (single or multiple records or rows)
- Reporting an application outage or error (e.g., an application is not available or there is a processing error when one attempts a specific process).
- Requesting a user account security role change (e.g., allowing an existing staffer to approve contracts up to $50,000).
- Adding to or altering an application work flow (e.g., routing an approved department contract to the central procurement team for final approval or processing).

Work items such as the ones listed above typically require IT change controls, or specific processes and testing to perform material changes to systems or applications. Most IT audits require the CIOs to document all material changes to the production systems, especially anything within or interfacing with the financial systems. In addition, there are mature systems for IT help desk and IT change control functions today. Some vendors provide both functions in a single application. My team uses a system from Microsoft that provides both.

So—back to the IT change control discussion. SLAs are different and typically shorter for tickets that are not IT change controls. This is because they take less time and are much less complex. The differences between an enterprise ticket with and without a formal IT change control are illustrated in the following examples:

- IT support ticket #3022 requests instructions on how to approve an invoice and route it via the work flow to a supervisor for approval if the invoice value differs and, as a result, so does the approver. This ticket would most likely be categorized as a severity 3 ticket, assigned to a technician or support resource (functional or business) and assigned a target resolution time of four to eight business hours.
- IT support ticket #6011 requests a bulk data change. Update the vendor code from ORCL to IBM for all purchases between January 1, 2013, and the current date as a result of a company acquisition. This ticket would most likely be categorized as a severity 2 or 3 ticket (depending on the urgency), assigned to a technician or support resource (technical), and assigned a target resolution time of five days as a result of the need to take the change through a formal IT change control. Formal change controls typically include the following high-level steps: (1) analyze, (2) design, (3) implement, (4) test, and (5) migrate to production.

In addition to having SLAs for specific requests, IT departments usually maintain target SLAs on system uptime for key systems. Exhibit 4.5 is an uptime SLA example for production systems across key infrastructure and applications.

Service	Uptime SLA	Time Objective	Down Time/ Maintenance
Network	99.5%	24/7 availability 24/7 support	3.6 hours/month (nonbusiness)
Applications	99.5% Day to Day 99.5% PeopleSoft Ceridian 98.0% Salesforce	24/7 availability Business hours support	3.6 hours/month (nonbusiness)
E-mail	99.5%	24/7 availability Business hours support	3.6 hours/month (nonbusiness)
Internet	99.5%	24/7 availability Business hours support	3.6 hours/month (nonbusiness)
Phones	99.5%	24/7 availability Business hours support	3.6 hours/month (nonbusiness)

Exhibit 4.5   Company A: System Uptime SLAs

The negotiation of SLA terms varies by service, vendor (including size and scope), and culture within an organization. In my experience, the following holds true for SLAs and externally contracted services:

- The larger vendors are harder to negotiate favorable SLAs with, including penalties, unless you're prepared to spend a significant amount of money with them annually.
- Web site and application hosting vendors commonly offer four nines (99.99 percent) of system uptime, and some of the more aggressive or nimble ones actually offer five nines (99.999 percent) uptime. In my experience, the vendors who are heavily leveraging virtualization technologies for many components (e.g., network, security, servers, and load balancers) have a higher probability of providing higher system uptimes.
- Smaller or regional vendors are easier to negotiate terms with, including SLAs and penalties, especially if they're competing against a big-name vendor. This is because they want the business more and the fees would represent a larger percentage of their annual revenue than they would with a large vendor like HP Enterprise Services, IBM, or Oracle.
- Larger vendors offer stability, standardized terms, and less flexibility in negotiating SLAs and in other key terms.
- Smaller vendors are much more flexible in contract negotiations, changes to key terms, and SLAs. I've actually had success in defining a set of aggressive SLAs from scratch that the vendor agreed to and also committed to pay if it didn't meet the SLA thresholds. With flexibility, however, comes risk—in lack of standardized processes, technologies, support techniques, and staff fault tolerance. The trick is to find the right organization—one that's mature and large enough to have more standardized processes but is still flexible on terms, SLAs, and penalties.

Annual Staff and Customer Surveys

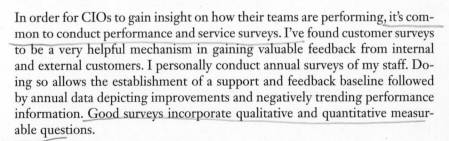

In order for CIOs to gain insight on how their teams are performing, it's common to conduct performance and service surveys. I've found customer surveys to be a very helpful mechanism in gaining valuable feedback from internal and external customers. I personally conduct annual surveys of my staff. Doing so allows the establishment of a support and feedback baseline followed by annual data depicting improvements and negatively trending performance information. Good surveys incorporate qualitative and quantitative measurable questions.

What follows is a sample survey with some questions I've used in the past. Adjust as appropriate for your organization. If you have a planning or polling team, solicit its advice, because it can offer best practices in survey design.

Section 1: Preamble and Introductory Questions. It's important to state the purpose of the survey and whether the survey designer will share the information that's compiled with the participants. You'll get more responses and more honest answers if the survey designer states that the survey is anonymous. Avoid questions for which the answers, or combinations of answers, could provide a window into the individual taking the survey. Use multiple-choice questions when appropriate for greater accuracy and easier reporting. Open-ended questions will require much more analysis, especially if the survey participant size is large. Also, avoid specific department names if a department is small or its name would easily identify an individual.

List the purposes of the survey, how frequently it will be done (if more than once), and what the responses will be used for. You may also get better responses and more participation if the participants believe that they will benefit in the future from providing input. I usually edit the responses and share them with the staff after the survey is closed and fully analyzed and the appropriate executives and subordinates have been briefed on the results and next steps. If there are obvious next steps to take, such as offering specific training to the staff, it may be very helpful to list any actions you'll take in the future as a result of the feedback from participants when you release or publish the results.

1. How many years have you been in the organization (tenure)? Hint for the survey developer: Use a multiple-choice list of year ranges (e.g., 0–2 years, 3–5 years, 6–10 years, 10 or more years).
2. What is your role? Hint: Develop an appropriate multiple-choice list, from administrative staff through managers and above, but don't spell out the top line titles, like *executive*, because the responses may be easy to use to identify a person.
3. At which office or location do you work? Hint: List the offices throughout your geographical landscape in a multiple-choice list. Be sure to list *home office*, if that's relevant to your workforce. (Example: Washington, D.C., Los Angeles, Toronto, London, home office).
4. What is your status (i.e., full-time or part-time)?

Section 2: IT Team Information (optional). Include information about what the IT team does, how it is organized, and what the focus areas are for each subunit (e.g., enterprise systems, network operations, PMO, web site, software development).

Section 3: Qualitative Questions. Ask a series of qualitative questions regarding the technologies and services provided, IT standards, the importance of specific technologies, the hours of support, and IT training. Adjust as appropriate for your organization.

1. Does the current computer standard meet your needs?
2. If not, what would you prefer to use as your main computer?
3. Does the organization's remote access solution provide ease of use and the necessary features for you to conduct your work out of the office?
4. If not, what would make remote working better?
5. Does the IT help desk provide flexible time around your schedule to work on issues that require in-person assistance?
6. Does the IT department provide sufficient IT training in the technologies and products we support?
7. What additional IT training would you like to see offered in the future?
8. Describe your IT support in the past year (poor, moderate, good, very good, excellent).
9. Do your IT service requests get solved quickly, and are your expectations met in terms of the published SLA?
10. Are IT policies, procedures, and standards clearly articulated on the company intranet site?
11. What IT policies require clarification?
12. What additional information would it be helpful to have IT communicate on the company intranet site?
13. What new IT services would be helpful to you in the future, and why?
14. What does IT do well?
15. What improvements can you suggest for IT?

Section 4: Quantitative Questions. Ask a series of quantitative questions that can be easily measured over time and by department.

Please rate the IT department in the areas in question on the following scale: 1 = strongly disagree, 2 = disagree, 3 = neutral, 4 = agree, 5 = strongly agree).

1. The IT team understands my business needs and demands.
2. IT provides solutions to my challenges.
3. The IT service provided is accurate and generally solves my issues on the first attempt.
4. The IT staff communicates professionally and politely.
5. I believe that the IT team is focused on results.
6. The IT team, including the help desk, provides timely responses to urgent requests.

7. The IT training staff provides effective training to my staff.
8. The IT team provides reliable technology and systems that support my job or role.
9. I understand the role of IT in this company.

Section 5: Overall IT Rating. I rate the IT department as follows: 1 = poor, 2 = moderate, 3 = good, 4 = very good, 5 = excellent.

There are a number of great survey tools available that can be integrated into your company's intranet and delivered via the Internet and e-mail. These tools are not expensive and allow for the multiyear design, development, analysis, and reporting of surveys. I highly recommend these staff surveys for CIOs.

Vendor Scorecarding

Another mechanism that can be helpful to CIOs and IT departments is the use of vendor scorecards. I find that vendor scorecards offer the following benefits:

- They develop and maintain an inventory of performance data and metrics for vendors—mainly strategic vendors (e.g., services and enterprise-class software and hardware), not commodity-based vendors.
- They drive improvements in performance for vendor services and deliverables.
- They foster relationships with strategic vendors by setting clear expectations, measuring interactions against those expectations, and communicating openly, professionally, and honestly.
- They foster team integration, bringing the technical and business staffs together to provide input and feedback on vendor performance.
- They provide a written record of vendor expectations, goals, issues, and accomplishments.

I typically compare the vendor feedback with our internal feedback (IT and business customers) and look for gaps in ratings. The larger the gaps between what the vendor thinks about its performance and what we think about its performance, the bigger a communications challenge we have.

The following is an example of a vendor scorecard:

Section 1. Vendor information, contacts, roles.

Section 2. Vendor input for key qualitative questions.

1. What top three accomplishments did you perform or assist with to drive success in the past year?

2. What, if any, challenges did you face during the past year? How would you change your approach to mitigate these challenges in the future and add perceived value?
3. What areas of improvement can you recommend to enhance your relationship with and add perceived value?

Section 3. Vendor input for key quantitative questions. Rank yourself from 1 to 5 (1 = low, 5 = high).
1. Responsiveness and availability
2. Quality of deliverables and work
3. Customer service orientation
4. Accuracy of work
5. Value for the investment
6. Professionalism in communication (open, consistent, effective)
7. Innovative work approaches
8. Proactive recommendations to solve challenges
9. Understanding of company's business needs
10. Quality of working relationships with the company staff

Section 4. Company input (IT and business staff) for key qualitative questions.
1. What top three accomplishments did the vendor perform or assist with to drive success in the past year?
2. What, if any, challenges did the vendor face during the past year? How would you change its approach to mitigate these challenges in the future and add perceived value?
3. What areas of improvement can you recommend for the vendor to enhance its relationship with and add perceived value?

Section 5. Company input (IT and business staff) for key quantitative questions. Rank the vendor from 1 to 5 (1 = low, 5 = high).
1. Responsiveness and availability
2. Quality of deliverables and work
3. Customer service orientation
4. Accuracy of work
5. Value for the investment
6. Professionalism in communication (open, consistent, effective)
7. Innovative work approaches
8. Proactive recommendations to solve challenges
9. Understanding of company's business needs
10. Quality of working relationships with the company staff

Section 6. List or describe the positive points of vendor performance.

Section 7. List or describe suggested recommendations for vendor improvement.

Section 8. Tabulate the results and report the final performance. Companies can get creative on the weighting of each question or section so that the final rating is an automated calculation and not subjective. I recommend using ratings that are descriptive (*poor, moderate, good, very good, excellent*) rather than simply a numbered scale.

Section 9. Signatures. I require signatures on all vendor scorecards from internal IT and business staff who provide input to the survey as well as a line management executive from the vendor. This ensures that when we deliver the results to the vendor, they will be read and acknowledged by a member of the senior executive team (vice president or higher).

I asked my executive and CIO expert group for their thoughts about service and about SLAs and how they define service targets and measure results. Their answers are eloquently stated in the CIO survey that follows.

CIO SURVEY

Do you use formal SLAs for key IT services, including help desk statistics tracking?

- Yes. However, the importance of and emphasis on this information is less important than it was five years ago. Today the business cares about the IT business scorecard and not IT-focused metrics in particular. The scorecard is shared on a monthly basis, but most business executives are most concerned about the initiatives that will affect their teams directly.
—*Joel Schwalbe, CIO, CNL Financial Group*

- Yes. Key applications have service level targets. We monitor service levels and report on them each month. It is the basis for discussions about areas that need attention. There are no penalties (other than hard feelings) if service levels are missed.
—*John Sullivan, CIO, American Chemical Society*

- Yes. We are using these statistics to measure our outsource vendor's performance.
—*A. Murat Mendi, CIO, Ulkar Holding*

What benefits do SLAs bring to your organization?

- SLAs provide a basis for providing adequate service levels to the business.
- As the business changes and grows, SLAs are the basis for changing the service level required for the new business.
- SLAs enable me to manage my resources across all three classes of IT expenses: lights on, expanding a service incrementally, and transforming a service exponentially.

—*Jay Seagren, Sr. Manager, Enterprise Systems, Pew Charitable Trusts*

- Customer satisfaction
- Performance improvements globally
- Benchmarking

—*Ray Barnard, SVP and CIO, Fluor*

- I have not been a strong advocate of SLA-based management, preferring relationship and leverage and the ability to tune a partnership in progress, but some of our newer outsourced operating agreements advocate for SLA-based metrics. The benefit to me remains to be determined.

—*Martin Gomberg, former CIO; SVP and Global Director, Business Protection, A&E Networks*

What percentage do you measure against (ideally, monthly) regarding meeting target response and resolution times to issues or tickets submitted?

Priority	Service
Critical	Respond within 15 minutes. 98% of tickets expected to meet target.
High	Respond within 1 hour. 95% of tickets expected to meet target.
Medium	Respond within 4 hours. 93% of tickets expected to meet target.
Low	Respond within business days. 90% of tickets expected to meet target.

—*Joel Schwalbe, CIO, CNL Financial Group*

Priority	Service
Severity 1	Resolve within 24 hours. 100% of tickets expected to meet target.
Severity 2	Resolve within 5 days. 99% of tickets expected to meet target.
Severity 3	Resolve within 30 days. 98% of tickets expected to meet target.

(Continued)

CIO SURVEY (*Continued*)

- I personally monitor this monthly, but the help desk manager and technology director monitor this daily.

—Phil Redmond, Managing Director, IT, Humane Society

How can you use SLAs to improve IT services? How are they communicated in your organization?

- Measuring all responses allows us to adjust personnel when and where necessary to improve the delivery of our services. We communicate how we are doing to IT personnel during our monthly departmental meeting and to management during monthly executive committee meetings and to all employees during town hall meetings.

—Carol F. Knouse, SVP and COO, EduTuit Corporation

- Set team goals to maintain the same SLA at a lower cost or improve the SLA at the same cost.

—Joshua R. Jewett, SVP and CIO, Family Dollar Inc.

- They assist with the management of expectations so that users know what services and service levels we provide and can gauge their expectations for assistance and service based on them in an objective manner. Our SLAs are posted on our intranet and also provided in a written document to the users when they buy data-center or managed services.

—Ed Anderson, International CIO, World Vision International

Do you benchmark your IT organization against others regarding SLAs? If so, why?

- No. We have little access to SLAs of other organizations. We would love to see industry standards for SLAs with third-party vendors, since it would help us hew to the norm. Today we often are guessing and probing to see what the vendor will bear.

—Dale Polekoff, CIO, Jacob Stern & Sons Inc.

- No, but I would be interested in doing so if there was a reliable body or organization that could accurately be compared to another.

—John Sullivan, CIO, American Chemical Society

What Did I Do to Prepare?

It's interesting to write a chapter about customer service and improvements on data that's collected both internally and benchmarked externally because so many people have different perspectives on what *service* is. As I researched this chapter and interviewed CIOs, it became obvious to me that the preponderance of research about service and SLAs was written from the contractual perspective (i.e., how to build SLAs and penalties into your contracts with vendors). The information within those documents was pretty consistent, and that's why so many of the IT service contracts we sign have boilerplate agreements with base SLAs and penalties now.

This is not so much the case on the internal SLA and measurement side, and it's definitely hard to find credible data on internal SLAs and benchmarks against other industries or organizations. For this reason, when I reviewed the internal SLAs from my CIO experts, they covered a wide range with little consistency—except on the response rates for the severity 1 and 2 issues. The rest of the feedback was like an international deck of cards.

The following outlines what I've done in the last decade regarding service-oriented frameworks, surveys, and SLAs:

- As part of my vendor management strategy, I have a section that includes target SLAs and penalties. I utilize this material every time I contract with a vendor for services, hosting, and so on. Over the years, I've used the materials from IT advisory services like Forrester Research and beneficial contract SLAs as updates to my vendor SLA portfolio of terms.
- I've designed and deployed internal SLAs, and I measure against them on a monthly basis in order to set standards of performance and then look for opportunities to improve upon them. I also publish my SLAs on the company intranet, including the measurements of monthly performance against targets—both response and resolution.
- I separate enterprise-class system SLAs from traditional IT help desk SLAs, because the types of service requests vary greatly.
- I conduct annual surveys of our customers to find out what we're doing well and what we need to do differently or improve upon. Organizations that are transparent and aren't afraid to learn and grow will publish the results of their annual surveys for full transparency.
- I scorecard a subset of my strategic vendors on an annual basis. The goals are simple for this process: reduce gaps in expectations between the customer and the vendor and improve performance for the investment.

Recommendations

My recommendations for this chapter are as follows:

- Leverage your IT advisory research firm for information on SLAs. Compare and contrast best practices and recommendations to what you have and adjust as necessary to improve them and put your company in a better position.
- Research companies that provide customer service outsourcing services: Alpine Access, Convergys, LiveOps, Teleperformance, TeleTech, West Corporation, and Sitel. They provide a combination of inbound and outbound services, including customer service, sales and acquisitions, collection, and other back-office functions.
- Check out www.surveymonkey.com. This is a great, inexpensive survey tool that companies can use to customize surveys and deliver or integrate them in a variety of ways. For information on more formal survey technology, consult your IT advisory research firm.
- If you don't include recommended contract SLA information within your vendor management strategy, start building a set of desired language-by-contract-services types. Start by listing the types of IT services your vendors provide, desired SLAs and penalties, current SLAs and penalties, and termination clauses. You can use the final document for new contracts and for negotiating improved terms for any renewal contracts. Poll your financial or contract system to find out what contracts will be due within the next six months and start the process sooner than later.
- Start scorecarding your vendors on your terms, not theirs. Many progressive and mature vendors scorecard their customers, but the wording and questions may not be what you're looking for; they're usually designed for the vendors. I only score strategic vendors and not commodity vendors. Commodity vendors are the vendors I can replace relatively easily (e.g., for computers or printers). Feel free to use my scorecard and modify it as you see fit.
- Deploy SLAs internally for your business customers and staff. Set achievable levels for response and resolution of the necessary severity levels that best match your business culture. If possible, integrate your SLAs into your IT help desk and IT change control system so that they become one. This is because all help desk tickets should have an SLA with a response and resolution target. Some of those tickets will turn into IT change controls. It's easier to manage the transition from ticket to change control and maintain SLA

information within one system. I utilize an integrated Microsoft solution.

- Publish or otherwise communicate the SLA targets, measure performance against those targets within your IT help desk ticketing system, and publish the results on a monthly basis. Doing so establishes transparency with your customers and gives you a very public means by which to strive for improvements.

- Research some of the new cloud-based service and support systems on the market. Salesforce.com has a new cool service called Service Cloud that integrates with its CRM software solution, integrates with social media channels and sites, and can communicate with customers via mobile devices—including the potential for video conferencing on some devices. The help desk system application market is in the midst of a significant transformation from applications that are installed in a company's data center to being deployed and integrated in the cloud.

Notes

1. Henry W. Longfellow, Inspirational Quotes, www.inspirational-quotes.info/success-quotes .html (accessed August 1, 2012).
2. Josh Bernoff, "Competitive Strategy in the Age of the Customer," Forrester Research, June 6, 2011.
3. Ibid.
4. Bobby Cameron, "CIOs Must Become Customer-Obsessed," Forrester Research, June 22, 2011.
5. Chip Gliedman, "CIOs: Step Up and Support Your Company's Customers," Forrester Research, November 11, 2011.
6. Ibid.
7. Lynn Greiner and Lauren Gibbons Paul, "SLA Definitions and Solutions," *CIO* magazine, August 8, 2007, www.cio.com/article/print/128900 (accessed August 27, 2012).
8. Ibid.

CHAPTER 5
Today's CIO

The Teacher to the C-Suite

The way to gain a good reputation, is to endeavor to *be* what you desire to appear.

—SOCRATES[1]

CIOs today are the primary educators of all things IT for the C-suite. The technology trends that affect organizations today are being discussed in boardrooms, at watercoolers, and in offices throughout the organization, not just in the IT department. Because of cloud computing, social media, and the consumerization of IT, business professionals no longer are beholden to IT to turn up a new service, launch a new social media feed, or connect a personal device to the institution's systems, most commonly e-mail and messaging.

As a result, there are many different interpretations of the complexity and ease of implementation regarding many of the technology trends changing the landscape across the globe today. CIOs must be at the forefront and engage in meaningful conversations with the appropriate professionals, from business and office professionals to the C-suite to the boardroom, so that decision makers have accurate information about the ease of turning up a new service as well as the risks, the integration requirements, the support costs, and the security implications.

CIOs today must be the teachers to the C-suite. In addition to fulfilling our day jobs, we've evolved to become executive educators—and just in time, before half of our budgets are moved outside IT by 2020. We must become better influencers of technology strategy, spending, and support. This chapter provides some insights into that challenge.

Gaps in Expectations between CIOs and CEOs and Other C-Level Executives

CIOs today still have an expectation gap in terms of what they'd like their roles to be, what they were hired to do, and what they end up actually doing. In the first edition, I researched this topic and found that the gaps that existed several years ago still persist today. Three of my executive recruiting experts described their thoughts on the most common gaps among CEOs, COOs, and CIOs:

> CEOs often want a CIO who is visionary and who is strategic, yet most often they value and emphasize the need for their CIO to work on tactical initiatives. Many CIOs do not feel that they are being tapped for their strategic ability.
>
> —*Beverly Lieberman, Halbrecht Lieberman Associates*

> I have found the most common gaps to be the following: (1) how long it takes and how much it costs to implement new systems that can help create a competitive edge, and (2) the lack of agreement and consensus around the prioritization of technology-oriented projects.
>
> —*Eric J. Sigurdson, Russell Reynolds Associates*

> Business process change. A CEO may want his or her CIO to bring the company through a major business model change. However, if the support and messaging are not clear and delivered from the top, the CIO will have an extremely difficult time pushing through the change at the business process level. Most CEOs truly believe they want to hire a strategic, revenue-generating CIO. However, once on board, the CIO spends all his time putting out fires and never truly gets to the strategic work.
>
> —*Martha Heller, Heller Search Associates*

When I speak with CIOs and IT executives from other companies and sectors, I often ask them the same question: "Are you operating in a strategic IT environment?" More often than not, the answer is no. Although most CIOs desire to be strategic and are hired to be strategic, they usually work at the operational and tactical level most of the time. I have found this to be true in my career as well.

Educating the C-Suite

Educating the C-suite is an opportunity to build relationships, enhance trust, and educate at the same time. My research and my interactions with other CIOs across the globe lead me to believe that a winning combination of narrowing the CEO-CIO gap and changing the direction of effort from operational to strategic is based on the following:

- Teaching the C-suite and the CEO in particular is done through influence over time.
- Relationships between the CIO and other C-level executives play a very important role in moving from operational and tactical to strategic IT. Spend time nurturing these relationships.
- Formal relationships are based on trust and respect.
- Respect is achieved through known external and internal perceptions of knowledge, leadership, and accomplishments. You must market yourself and your team's accomplishments. You need to become an internal sales executive for ideas and accomplishments and an external adviser who shares their experiences, best practices, and lessons learned with others outside your organization.
- Education is a fine art, which is why many simply don't do it well. A lecture is not educating. Educating is the fine art of influence and sharing of knowledge in a nonthreatening manner. CIOs need to remember that CEOs are some of the most egotistical professionals on the planet. Making bold recommendations and lecturing about the need to use technology A or B to solve a business problem could have a very negative effect and result in a nontrusting relationship. The best professors I've ever had taught me a lot. They *showed* me that *caring* about why one does something, teaches someone, or recommends a solution is more important than the lesson itself. Thus, teaching the C-suite is a delicate proposition. Many CEOs might not take kindly, especially in front of others, to the fact that their subordinates are smarter than they are. It's way too threatening. Balance and tone are the keys.
- If you influence the C-suite, the C-suite will influence the CEO. Spend less time trying to teach the CEO personally and more time politely educating the other executives about your ideas and how certain technologies can solve their business problems. These executives will do the heavy lifting by advising the CEO and supporting your position. Suggestions in numbers fare better than lone propositions.

Some pundits are calling for the end of the CIO role as a result of the new disruptive technologies like cloud computing, mobile, and social media, because these people think that businesses can provision and use technology without needing IT to procure, provision, and service it for them. According to Forrester Research, "These changes bring a unique opportunity for CIOs to step up and lead their technology organizations into the world of empowered business technology."[2]

Empowered business technology (EBT) is "the technology approach where enabling technology innovation is embedded in the business while IT provides *just enough* centralized coordination and oversight for enterprise goals."[3] Just think how many businesses are leveraging cloud-based marketing tools to drive social media campaigns—all without IT oversight and funding from the central IT budget.

Business leaders and CIOs need to make technology decisions together now more than ever, especially in an EBT environment. Forrester describes the following five actions that are attributes of the empowered CIO:

1. Shift to empowerment, empowering the employees and customers to solve problems, through a myriad of technology channels, including mobile and social.
2. Develop a reputation as a dynamic service provider. The CIO is becoming a service provider who "orchestrates technology service providers," including in the cloud, to serve the business.
3. Adopt a federated organizational model. The CIO will still retain governance of enterprise technologies and integration between cloud and enterprise solutions, but let the business drive the embedded technologies at the business level.
4. Provide value through governance, sourcing, and innovation.
5. Become a COO in order to cocreate solutions with the business and only own through governance the enterprise infrastructure and integration.[4]

Educating the CEO and the C-suite can be done through informal meetings, formal discussions at management committee meetings, strategic meetings with vendors who are candidates to assist with key strategic IT and business initiatives, and one-on-one discussions with peer business unit leaders and the CEO. If the culture is right, scorecards may be helpful for updates on key initiatives, projects, and policy recommendations in group meetings.

Creating a High-Performing IT Team through Education

Creating high-performing teams requires formal and informal education, mentoring, training frameworks, policies, and procedures. CIOs today must do a better job of educating their technical and business workforce through a targeted and deliberate approach. No longer can we rely solely on vendor training. We must partner closely with our business partners, create a training strategy, implement it, and monitor the performance for effectiveness. This chapter provides some insights on creating high-performing teams.

Formal Educational Programs and Degrees

Formal academic educational programs can add value to traditional and targeted IT training and certification programs. Academic programs are typically good at providing general knowledge over a long period. Chapter 6 discusses the academic background that executive recruiters prefer for CIOs today.

For those candidates and aspiring CIOs, look to augment an undergraduate degree with an advanced degree, and do it before you apply for the CIO role. Sitting CIOs who have come up the experience ladder before graduate degrees for executives became popular are safe, because they have achieved the role with hard work, IT results, and experience.

For the few CIOs who are interested in a higher level of education, participating in a master's or doctoral degree can be a difficult career balance, since the CIO role is very demanding. The CIOs I know who have taken that plunge are preparing for their next careers as academic professors. This option is likely to be the lowest probability for sitting CIOs, because of the time commitment and the potential to interfere with the role of running IT in their companies. Fortunately, there are other options for educational expansion.

IT Training Courses: Targeted Instruction

I'm a big fan of formal IT training courses, especially when they are targeted toward instruction that will benefit the participant in an existing or upcoming technology or project. This is the most common form of IT training and the most likely for those who have not yet reached the pinnacle of the CIO role. Courses that can apply to all IT professionals include project management, security, and methodologies (e.g., ITIL, COBIT).

CIOs and their managerial subordinates need to have proactive training plans for their staffs that link into their organizations' technologies, goals, and projects. Be deliberate. A typical formal IT training course runs from two days to a week, if it is done right. Classic courses today are networking, business intelligence, cloud-based integration, social media marketing, software development, storage area network (SAN) management, virtualization, and statistical analysis and modeling.

Certification: Does It Matter?

Some IT pros believe that certification is the only way to go in IT training and education. I'm not in that camp, but I do think it adds value. Learning a technology and using it soon on an institutional project is the most valuable execution of IT training. Passing a test is an afterthought, in my opinion. Earlier in my career I pursued certification. In my experience as an academic adjunct, the courses that were for certification focused more on how to take a test than on learning the technology to apply it in a practical setting.

That said, there are several IT roles for which certification is helpful and recommended: network engineers, system administrators, software developers, SAN administrators, security professionals (including CISOs), and virtual server and VDI engineers. These roles are often at the heart of what keeps IT systems operational, but they are not typically required to become a CIO. They're helpful for roles below the CIO. CIOs focus on strategy, security, governance, methodologies, policies, learning the business, relationships with business partners, contract and vendor management and negotiation, risk management, compliance, and leadership. There are only a few courses and certifications that fill that group of required skills, and they are typically offered by very specific and well-known providers and universities.

Mentoring

I discussed mentoring a bit in the first edition. Mentors are usually really special people who have great insight, solid experience to draw from, and a broad set of professional and personal contacts, and they are bright, energetic, and generous in giving their time and advice. Good mentors are also extremely rare and hard to find. I've been fortunate in my career to find a few mid- and senior-level professionals who have served as mentors to me and who guided the development of my technical and business skills.

I had my first mentor fairly early in my professional career, when I was in my mid-20s. She was a mid- to senior-level consulting manager who had exceptional client management, project management, and communication skills. For some reason, she decided to take me under her wing and guide my career, possibly because I was always very energized and positive about working with our customers and solving their problems. She guided me in developing and honing my client management and communications skills. This was one of the most important boosts for my career at the time.

Back then, as today, being technical or having business acumen was not enough to be put into a leading and face-to-face position with a client or prospective customer. Communication skills, polish, presentation style, and other "soft" skills are just as important as the "hard" technical skills in today's IT market. I remember many instances of practicing presentations with her until she was satisfied that I would deliver them right. Her advice still stands in my memory today: Present what you know and target the script to your audience.

My second and third mentors were ex-consultants who served as executives in the organizations where I also worked. Both were knowledgeable and influential. After developing closer professional relationships with them, I started to have more open and honest conversations on a variety of topics, ranging from skill development to business knowledge and even personal issues. I found, as an indirect result of my closer association with these two mentors, that I learned most by observing them in a professional environment.

Expanding that to observe others in action, I learned what to do and, infrequently, what not to do by watching them and other executives and visionaries in leadership roles. When I wanted clarification on something, I asked for it, and since we had established trusted relationships, the information and conversations usually flowed freely in both directions.

That said, I believe that human beings learn in one of three ways: (1) preparing for the task at hand, doing the research, spending time on a well-thought-out approach for a project or product, and yielding a successful outcome; (2) watching someone else make a mistake; or (3) making the mistake themselves. I prefer the first and second options. Finding a professional mentor who can influence and advise you, directly or indirectly, with intent is as important as all the other professional and career development methods rolled up into one powerful and effective package.

So how does one find a mentor? For starters, ask for help from someone who is influential, knowledgeable, reputable, and interested in you—someone you think you can build a long-term relationship with. Some people who are searching for mentors simply get lucky and get offers from them. Others have to seek them out and convince them that they're worth the effort and that the relationship will evolve to be bidirectional in time and value. All of my mentors to date have been at a higher level in experience and seniority. I think that this is important, since mentors should have refined skills and deep experience that the mentees most likely don't have but desire. The following mechanisms may also lead to finding a good mentor:

- Networking with professionals beyond your current grade or level—inside and outside your current organization. Exposure is key to meeting the right mentor.
- When you find someone you respect and think you can learn from, ask for guidance.
- Academic environments are great places to search for a mentor, especially since colleges and universities are geared toward higher learning and helping students to grow.

- Search out organizations and programs that offer mentoring services. Some are free while others are fee-based.
- Look at management training programs within your organization and apply for the ones that increase your interaction with senior management executives. Some companies have well-defined programs for mentoring new executives or rising stars. During my tenure at a Fortune 200 financial services firm, I went through an excellent 20-month senior management training program, and the experience and executive level contacts I made were invaluable.

According to an *Inc.* magazine article, it usually takes some research and time to identify multiple candidates for mentors. According to Kathy Kram, an associate professor of organizational behavior at Boston University's School of Management and the author of *Mentoring at Work*, "I think people really ought to think in terms of multiple mentors instead of just one." She suggests that not all mentors have to be high-ranking executives. Rather, "Peers can be an excellent source of mentorship."[5]

In a different *Inc.* magazine article, the author suggests the following steps to finding a great mentor:

- Know yourself. Think about where you are and where you want to be.
- Be proactive. Develop a plan and ask before waiting to be asked. Also, do some research before you start lobbing dumb questions at a prospective mentor. Smart people (and mentor candidates) don't like stupid questions, and they tend to cater to individuals who crave answers to the right questions that have sound motivations.
- Ask for referrals. Friends and colleagues can be a great source.
- Keep an open mind about who your mentor might be. A mentor doesn't necessarily have to be a heavy hitter or power player. He or she should be knowledgeable and have a desire to help others, specifically in the traits and skills you want to improve.
- Identify alternative mentors. Never put all your eggs in one basket. Mentors can come from a variety of places, both business and nonbusiness sources.
- Know what you want to achieve from the relationship.
- Think about people who have been your mentors in the past. We've all had mentors in our lives, whether we realize it or not. Review the pros and cons of your experiences and apply what worked or was valuable in the past to the future.[6]

It is noteworthy that the mentors (both mine and others') I've met in my career usually also had a mentor, or several mentors, in their lives and appear to be eager to pay it forward. I've adopted the pay-it-forward strategy as well and am currently working with at least two mentees. It's quite rewarding, and I highly recommend that sitting CIOs and other executives give it a try.

Informal Learning and Collaboration

I'm a big fan of learning informally. In today's social media environment, the staff does this on its own and with little guidance. Internal social media, knowledge management, and collaboration tools in an organization can clearly drive informal learning by giving individuals the technical ability to connect the dots and find information quickly. Forrester Research identifies nine steps in an informal learning strategy (see Exhibit 5.1).[7]

In the last five or so years, my teams and I have been engaged in informal learning through Microsoft SharePoint, Salesforce.com, Chatter, custom knowledge management solutions, and informal brown-bag sharing sessions in order to share knowledge, lessons learned, and best practices. I've also

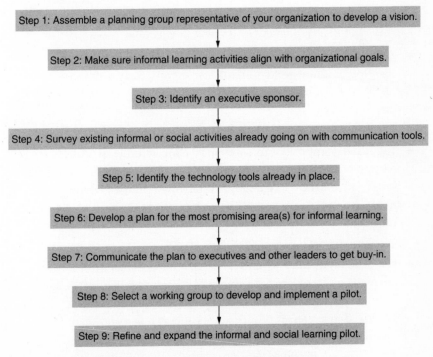

Exhibit 5.1   Essential Steps in an Informal Learning Strategy
Source: Forrester Research, Inc.

found that asking the staff to conduct learning sessions, and essentially teach others, helps them to refine their own communication skills. Win-win.

I asked my executive and CIO expert group for their thoughts about educating the C-suite and its staff. Their answers are eloquently stated in the CIO survey that follows.

CIO SURVEY

Do you believe that the role of the CIO today is as a teacher to other executives in the C-suite?

- Yes. I think that other executives can learn a lot from a knowledgeable CIO. Because we typically have involvement in all functional areas of an organization, I believe that we sometimes understand the interdependence between business units better than the key executives who head up those areas [do]. I believe we are much less territorial and proprietary than many other executives.
—*Carol F. Knouse, SVP and COO, EduTuit Corporation*

- Yes, if they are willing to listen. Executives have often made up their minds about certain things before consulting with those who might have more insight. I think this is the nature of many highly driven people.
—*Dale Polekoff, CIO, Jacob Stern & Sons Inc.*

- Yes. It's very important to continually educate other executives on potential opportunities for improvement, whether or not they involve technology. Credibility is established primarily through relationship and delivery (delivering on commitments such as SLAs and projects).
—*Joel Schwalbe, CIO, CNL Financial Group*

- Yes, absolutely. The CIO and his team are masters of project management, process reengineering, call centers and help desks, business analysis and analytics, and of course technology. The key is to serve as a source of best practices and to teach and share this knowledge across the enterprise.
—*David Swartz, CIO, American University*

How to you educate other executives on the technology changes and strategies required to meet institutional goals?

- If you know your business, you explain how these emerging technologies or strategies can help them to innovate, improve their existing operations by providing growth and better productivity, and prepare to successfully enter new markets or develop new products.
- A CIO's effectiveness at the table should be tied directly to the success of the business. Let's face it, even the business that outwardly appears to have no ties to technology does rely on technology to survive and to thrive. A [company] president once told me that "technology may be seen as merely a tool, but it is critical to the success of my business."

—*Earl Monsour, Director, Strategic Information Technologies, Maricopa Community College District*

- In my case, introducing new and novel technologies with peers is something I do very informally. I routinely meet with peers at corporate [headquarters], travel with field operations, and attend departmental functions. It is in these informal settings that seeds can best be planted. With respect to larger and more strategic decisions, it has been my experience that peers will defer to my judgment on areas deemed to be on my turf—core application and infrastructure investment, for example. While I operate in their province, however, it is more important to find common ground, outline the win-win, and gain their acceptance of the importance and relevance of the change. I should also add that it is often they (other executives) who bring challenging ideas to me and my team for innovations in their areas of specialty.

—*Joshua R. Jewett, SVP and CIO, Family Dollar Inc.*

- By delivering solutions that meet all the drivers and continuously promoting the IT function in terms of value delivered, efficiencies gained, and sustainability of solutions. It can certainly be risky to anticipate the need of the business ahead of an actual question, but nothing engenders trust and partnership more than being a couple of steps ahead of the business leaders and coming with a potential solution to a forming need. Plus, it puts IT in a position of strength and prevents having to react to business needs and compress timelines.

(Continued)

CIO SURVEY (*Continued*)

- The best measure of effectiveness will be when we can stop saying "the business" and "IT" as two separate entities. Nobody segregates other corporate functions away from the business. Why should IT be separated away from procurement, legal, finance, sales, distribution, operations, and so on?
—*Peter Classon, Partner, LiquidHub Inc.*

I conduct three main activities in this area:

- At executive committee meetings, I will do a presentation on a particular technology topic that I believe would be beneficial for the organization.

- I meet personally with each key executive every month. As part of that meeting, we discuss his or her particular issues and challenges, and I will discuss what we can do to help with the application of technology to solve a particular business problem or to help grow the business.

- At town hall meetings, I typically bring in third parties to exhibit the latest technologies, like mobile applications, so that all employees can adopt a mindset of how technology can improve the way they do their jobs.
—*Carol F. Knouse, SVP and COO, EduTuit Corporation*

What are your best methods for providing leadership and technology training for your IT subordinates?

- Cross-training.

- Giving people the ability to work in other areas. Do not just silo them to their skill sets. Develop a yearly plan with each staffer asking about other areas of interest and let him or her work in that area.
—*Sanjay Khatnani, President, J2 Solutions*

- Leadership by example.

- On the job opportunities.

- Business partner presentations and training.

- Third-party *educational programs.*

—Joshua R. Jewett, SVP and CIO, Family Dollar Inc.

- Creating a simple IT strategy that aligns with the business and exposes the IT team to the customers (so that the strategy is real to them), and having other C-levels share their views with the team and how they add value.

- Individual development plans for all IT staff that includes training that everyone should have, like SDLC, project management, initiation into the organization, common sense processes, and IT security, as well as training specific to the role the IT person is in. Example: A DBA should have training on its current product set, the tools associated with it, performance tuning, security, and other related items. An annual, predictable budget can be developed by position and reused as staff members change.

—Ed Anderson, International CIO, World Vision International

- For technology training for IT staff, on-the-job training is the most effective. Whenever we implement new technologies, we provide formal training to the key IT staffers before implementation, if at all possible. Ideally, the staff would have a chance to play with the technology in a test environment. Most important, we hire contractors who have done multiple implementations, who have the necessary expertise and experience, and who build extra time and costs in the contract to transfer knowledge throughout the project. In many cases, the internal IT staff does the actual keyboarding, as the consultant instructs. One of the final steps requires that the IT staffers involved in the project document the technology. Writing documentation reinforces what they have learned.

—Anne Topp, CIO, World Wildlife Fund

What Did I Do to Prepare?

In the last five years or so, I've focused on being the informal and formal teacher of the executives and subordinates under my charge. Influencing an executive peer or a higher-level executive is definitely a tricky proposition, because you don't want to appear arrogant or superior. The best CIO executive teachers I know are *influencers*—through safe conversations; vendor briefings; leading by example; and facilitating frequent meetings with staff, peers, and strategic leaders. They enjoy sharing information and learning.

The following is an outline of what I've done in the last decade to provide IT educational services to the CEO, other C-level executives, and my team:

- I've developed high-level training plans for each IT subunit and worked closely with my subordinates so that they can map out the necessary training for each of their staffers. I tend to budget for at least one IT training course per person and also include research- or project-oriented conferences for key staff members.
- I've introduced new technologies at all IT staff meetings and town halls, when appropriate, to educate the staff about what's being utilized or coming down the pike for certain high-target institutional initiatives.
- In conversations with the CEO, I like to take an opportunity in person and through e-mail to educate him or her on a possible technology strategy or tool that could benefit the organization. The key is to speak in business terms. I often reference third-party independent research to strengthen the support for what I'm trying to communicate, because it can reinforce best practices through external qualifications.
- I'm still evolving with regard to business transformation and the integration of cloud, mobile, and social tools that don't necessarily need IT to engage and use within a business. The CIO role is one of continual learning. We need to stay current on technological change, business and strategy changes, and external and disruptive drivers that make big changes in society and business possible. This process will take time, because the trends and changes affecting business today and decentralizing IT to the business are not mature but are still in the disruptive phase of business and market evolution.
- I like to publish the IT strategic plan and share it with my team. Depending on the culture, sharing the final document or strategy may be limited to IT and C-level executives as a result of some potentially confidential and prereleased strategies, weaknesses, and threats associated with an updated SWOT analysis. If at all possible, publish for all staff to see for full transparency.
- Continue learning: business, technology, and drivers of change. I like to leverage IT advisory research for tracking trends through investment dollars and follow up in more detail with demonstrations and discussions with the vendors who are leading those markets, sectors, and technologies.

Recommendations

As an academic doctoral candidate, a lifelong learning IT professional, and someone who values sharing knowledge and not hoarding it, I hope that this chapter and the recommendations are as helpful to the readers as they've been to me over the years. My recommendations for this chapter are as follows:

- Become a mentor if you're a CIO or a candidate CIO. Giving back is a leadership quality that will help aspiring CIOs rise to the rank of executive.
- Find a mentor if your title and professional status are predirector. It's very helpful, and with the right mentor, doors that you never believed were possible to open can open. Becoming a CIO and staying one is about leadership, performance, results, and relationships.
- Understand the gaps between executives and the lower levels in your organization and map out a strategy to close them. Communication and relationship building will most likely be at the center of the process.
- Sitting CIOs need to adjust to business transformation as decentralized IT spending in the business is happening, whether we like it or not. I just returned from the Salesforce.com Dreamforce event in San Francisco, and one of the executive presenters forecasted that IT spending in the business would outpace IT spending in the IT department by the end of the decade. If true, that's going to require CIOs to retool their approach for aligning IT with the business, since the business can now procure IT services and systems *without* IT as a result of the trends and disrupters happening in the market today.
- Create high-performing IT and business teams through deliberate training programs that blend academic, IT, certification, and business training. A training plan should be a deliverable that's a byproduct of an updated IT strategic plan and should help to align human capital to the institutional priorities and the tools and technologies that will be leveraged to meet their goals.
- Attend vendor demonstrations and discussions to learn about new technologies that are being developed specifically for mobile, cloud, and social technologies.
- Attend IT conferences to learn how other organizations are solving the challenges that you're wrestling with in your firm. Peer discussions across companies and sectors is a great way to learn and to teach. If you get an opportunity to present at an event, take it and start a lifelong trend of doing so. I aim for doing at least one public presentation or discussion per year, and typically in a diverse technical and business setting.

- Learn how to be an effective communicator. Knowing your audience is so important. IT professionals need to become comfortable speaking with peers, subordinates, and superiors in *their* language and at the right focal level. For those who are not comfortable presenting or discussing business and technology strategy with executives, including the C-suite, there are some great educational courses and programs that are designed to transform people into effective communicators. I believe that communication skills are one of the most important skills for CIOs today. Along with IT and business acumen, communication skills are essential for developing relationships with others, including executives. If you're not "in the zone" and feeling great about your communication skills, enroll in the best course you can find. Ensure that the course offers instruction with videotaping. Most professionals have no idea how they look when they present or communicate with others. A trained professional with a video camera can greatly assist with this essential feedback.

Notes

1. Socrates, www.inspirational-quotes.info/growth.html (accessed December 27, 2012).
2. Khalid Kark, Bobby Cameron, Marc Cecere, Nigel Fenwick, Chip Gliedman, and Craig Symons, "The Empowered BT CIO," Forrester Research, July 18, 2011.
3. Ibid.
4. Ibid.
5. Karen Dillon, "Finding the Right Mentor for You," *Inc.*, October 22, 2000, www.inc.com/articles/2000/10/14859.html (accessed October 1, 2012).
6. Jamie Walters, "Seven Tips for Finding a Great Mentor," *Inc.*, April 2, 2001, www.inc.com/articles/2001/04/22407.html (accessed October 1, 2012).
7. Claire Schooley, "Informal Learning Garners Acceptance as a Legitimate Learning Approach," Forrester Research, July 14, 2011.

PART TWO

The Modern-Day CIO

CHAPTER 6

What Executive Recruiters Are Looking for, from Consulting Experience to Leadership Skills

Leadership is the art of getting someone else to do something you want done because he wants to do it.

—Dwight D. Eisenhower[1]

I thought it would be as important in this edition as it was in the last to provide expertise and recommendations from some of America's top recruiting experts. I have selected regional, national, and international firms and individuals to ensure that the readers will receive the proper blend of executive recruiting insights to help them in either a first CIO quest or a repeated opportunity.

How to Get Noticed

Finding an executive recruiter who can help you in your career is not an easy task but one that takes a significant amount of time. It's about building a relationship with a person who knows your skills, accomplishments, and capabilities and who, when the time is right, can present you as a candidate to an employer for a top IT position. Relationships can take years to build. In my career, I've met most of my recruiting contacts through the following methods:

- By attending IT conferences and other events
- By doing speaking engagements

- As a byproduct of publishing an article or a book
- From introductions by mentors

Any way you cut it, executive recruiters should be part of your extended network, especially as your career advances. My network has actually shrunk since I started in IT 26 years ago. The reason is that the higher my role as a result of promotions or changing jobs, the more the scope and size of my network changed. Earlier, employees, peers, and vendors were my predominant business contacts. The higher my role became, the less I relied on employees and peers and the more I relied on business professionals outside IT, mentors, and executive recruiters to help me manage and develop my career.

Exhibit 6.1 highlights the key components of my network along with the importance of certain groups that have recently played an important role as I became a CIO and was selected for other CIO roles. Mentors, vendors (limited and most likely larger firms), business professionals, and executive recruiters have played a critical role in my career, with a focus on growth and opportunity.

The techniques for rising in the ranks within an organization differ from those for taking advantage of an opportunity in another organization. According to a CNN Money article, "The new currency at work is influence," which is the key to getting noticed and increasing your exposure.

Exhibit 6.1   Effective Networking Relationships

Contributing author Elaine Profeldt suggests four simple ways to be noticed and promoted:

1. Make upper management's priorities your priorities.
2. Be ahead of the trends.
3. Script small talk.
4. Volunteer for key committees.[2]

The minimum title or role required to get the attention of an executive recruiter is *manager*, but even better is *director* or *vice president*. I stress the *executive* in *executive recruiter* because there is a significant difference between a traditional recruiter (or head hunter, as this role is often called) and an executive recruiter. Executive recruiters recruit for *executive* leadership positions. These professionals are highly skilled, tapped into C-level leadership roles, and at the top tier of compensation as a result of the clientele they place. It's not uncommon for a good executive recruiter to receive compensation of between $50,000 and $80,000 for a solid CIO candidate. Certain sectors, such as financial, pay even more, well over $100,000 per individual.

Professional networking sites like LinkedIn can also help you get noticed by an employer or an executive recruiter, especially if you're at the right level: director, vice president, or higher. According to the *Washington Post*, LinkedIn boasts at least 150 million members in more than 200 countries. In addition, LinkedIn "reports that its hiring solutions are used by 82 Fortune 500 companies" and notes that executives from all of the Fortune 500 have profiles established on the social networking site.[3]

Social networking is not all roses and wine. While many expound the benefits of professional social networking sites, there are some disadvantages. First, sales representatives and account executives use these sites to dredge up new leads, often contacting members online in an attempt to sell a product or set up an introductory meeting. When I was on a site years ago, as a CIO, I found that more than 90 percent of contact initiated by other members was sales related. Simply put, it was a distraction for me and did not actually help me build or refine my network.

Direct access to sales professionals is why I do not have a LinkedIn profile today. I have opted instead for a concise web site online presence that details my career, expertise, publications, awards, and speaking engagements (past and future). A network is like a fine wine or aged bourbon: it improves with age in scope, size, and benefits. I found that my network increased in size and scope earlier in my career as I attempted to reach a broader audience than the significantly smaller one that is available to a C-level professional.

Only the individual themselves can tell when their networks are too small or too big. One piece of advice, though: if your network is consuming time, preventing productivity in your existing role, or not assisting your rise to your desired role, it's probably too big and broad and needs to be pruned.

Leading Generation Y and Mentoring

Regarding mentoring, sitting CIOs, who are often baby boomers, need to take a different approach to mentoring their Generation Y (Gen Y) IT professionals. According to Gerry McCartney, Purdue University's CIO and one of my CIO contributors to this book, "Manage expectations" and "State flat-out that if they do these certain things, they are going to be successful." Feedback is important to the Gen Y professional, and according to McCartney, "The immediacy of the feedback is the key."[4] CIOs should identify what motivates their team members, the candidates for future IT leaders and CIOs, and enforce that driver often so their employees have a sense of pride in their accomplishments.

I have been mentoring for more than 10 years now, often providing career insight and networking connections to multiple mentees at the same time. It's an important role for today's CIOs and one that should be repeated in history for the next generation. When I was a director at a Fortune 100 financial services firm, my mentor was instrumental in introducing me to executive recruiting resources that helped me climb in my career and eventually obtain the role and title of CIO. As a result, mentors are key—both for aspiring CIOs and for sitting CIOs. I firmly believe that sitting CIOs have an obligation to mentor capable, hardworking IT professionals who will someday replace us in our roles.

In this chapter, my distinguished group of executive recruiters provides answers that are intended to prepare sitting CIOs for their next career challenges as well as first-time CIO candidates. The recruiters are formally introduced here:

1.   Martha Heller, President, Heller Search Associates

2. Derek Wilkinson, Managing Director, Boyden Global Executive Search

3. Beverly Lieberman, President, Halbrecht Lieberman Associates

4. Kathryn Graham Shannon, Global Practice Managing Partner, Heidrick & Stuggles

EXECUTIVE RECRUITER SURVEY

What are the top 10 skills that CIOs need to have to be competitive today?

Business acumen	Change management
Relationship-building abilities	Team leadership
Strategic thinking	Global leadership
Technical acumen	Project management
The ability to innovate	The ability to meet with external clients

—Martha Heller, Heller Search Associates

Agility	A big-picture vision
A business support and customer service mentality	The ability to compare and contrast new technologies in ways that include growth, flexibility, feasibility, security, and ease of use
A sense of humor	
A balance of strategy and tactics	Leadership skills—up, down, sideways
A willingness to and deftness in speaking truth to power	Management skills—up, down, sideways
	Being an up-to-date, hands-on technologist

—Derek Wilkinson, Boyden Global Executive Search

Leadership	The ability to align IT with the mission of the CEO
The capability of building strong interpersonal relationships	
The ability to manage costs and work within constrained budgets	The capability of managing change
	The ability to innovate
A broad and deep understanding of IT	An understanding of trends and plans accordingly
A service orientation	A knowledge of outsourcing, SaaS, and the like

—Beverly Lieberman, Halbrecht Lieberman Associates

Business awareness	The ability to build strong relationships—inside and outside (e.g., vendors)
Communication skills	
Financial acumen	People management (being a mentor and a coach, attracting and retaining talent)
Innovativeness	
Technical acumen	Strategic thinking
	The ability to be a change agent
	Project management

—Kathryn Graham Shannon, Heidrick & Stuggles

These collective responses don't vary much from those in the first edition. I'm personally thrilled to see that my strong view that the CIO still needs to have a commanding understanding of technology is validated by every one of the recruiters.

What advice would you give to first-time CIO candidates as part of the recruiting process?

- Make sure you can talk about your accomplishments in business terms. It's not "I led the deployment of a single instance global SAP system." It's "I increased productivity by 20 percent and drove down costs by 10 percent through an IT strategy that included an SAP implementation."

—*Martha Heller, Heller Search Associates*

- Figure out how to get an early win that has an effect on the organization as a whole, and command respect through that. Also, being a team player with leadership from day one.

—*Derek Wilkinson, Boyden Global Executive Search*

- To be sure they ask good questions to draw out what is needed in a CIO. Listen and learn from everyone you meet.

—*Beverly Lieberman, Halbrecht Lieberman Associates*

- Learn the business and earn a seat at the table! Create value for your business partners and do it in a way that makes financial sense. Treat your people well and manage them uniquely—it's not one size that fits all. Keep your eye on the future as much as you keep your eye on today.

—*Kathryn Graham Shannon, Heidrick & Stuggles*

What are the most common gaps between what CEOs and COOs are looking for in a CIO and what a CIO can actually deliver?

- CEOs want a CIO who can be strategic and innovative and drive new growth. However, CIOs often inherit a messy infrastructure, a demoralized team, and a business community that is resistant to IT investment. It's the CIO paradox: "You were hired to be strategic, but you always wind up in the weeds."

—*Martha Heller, Heller Search Associates*

(Continued)

EXECUTIVE RECRUITER SURVEY (*Continued*)

- Fast, cheap, and good. Leaders want all three, and most CIOs can only deliver on two. Any CIO who can't manage that won't be able to stick for long.

—*Derek Wilkinson, Boyden Global Executive Search*

- CIOs do not always prepare senior management for the difficulty of implementing new systems and their time frames. As a result, "go live" dates are often not met.

—*Beverly Lieberman, Halbrecht Lieberman Associates*

- Not every CEO or COO is looking for the same thing, but more often than in the past, CEOs and COOs are looking for added value from their CIOs—not just maintaining the IT shop and keeping the lights on.

—*Kathryn Graham Shannon, Heidrick & Stuggles*

What are the top five areas of experience that CIOs need to have today?

- Leading a major transformation.

- Managing a global organization.

- Building a shared service organization.

- Reorganizing IT so that it is aligned with the business.

- Developing a strategy to provide business intelligence to the company's business leaders.

—*Martha Heller, Heller Search Associates*

- Experience in a business-side role (i.e., having only corporate headquarters experience is seen as limiting).

- Experience tackling a previously viewed insurmountable task or issue.

- Experience in completely redoing IT systems (knowing how "from soup to nuts").

- Experience in financial or auditing system overhaul and understanding.

- Experience in failing, learning from it, and recovering spectacularly.

—*Derek Wilkinson, Boyden Global Executive Search*

Wilkinson's responses remind me of several similar questions I was recently asked when interviewing for my current CIO position. Specifically, I was asked to provide an example of a previous failed project and detail my involvement, the lessons I learned, and how I'd do it differently. This is an invaluable question to think about. Have your answer fully prepared without pause.

- Outsourcing.
- Understanding centralized and decentralized organization models and how to deliver value in either scenario.
- Understanding the business drivers of the company.
- Understanding the ultimate customer and how to work on his or her behalf.
- Knowing how to work with matrix staff that is not geographically nearby—often people in different countries with different customs and work ethics.

—*Beverly Lieberman, Halbrecht Lieberman Associates*

Today, outsourcing is clearly a valuable skill for IT leaders. CIOs must know how to build an organization by core competency from the inside out and determine which functions are not core to the IT team and can be outsourced. In addition, I think back to when I was a principal consultant at PriceWaterhouseCoopers LLP and reflect on Lieberman's advice about geographically based staff from different cultures. Training on this one is helpful. PriceWaterhouse provided us with training on the cultural differences of team members and how to work better as a team even when there are significant philosophical and cultural differences among the team members. I ended up as an instructor in the firm, teaching consulting best practices, methodologies, ethics, and cultural diversity. It's some of the best training I've received in my life.

(Continued)

EXECUTIVE RECRUITER SURVEY (*Continued*)

- Delivering value creation to the business and through technology.
- Developing an IT strategy.
- Providing efficient and effective IT services.
- Developing strong IT leadership teams.
- Clearly defining the results achieved by IT tied to business goals.

—*Kathryn Graham Shannon, Heidrick & Stuggles*

How important is consulting experience for a first-time CIO, and why?

- High. Consulting experience, particularly if it comes at the beginning of a CIO's career, gives the candidate a foundation in SDLC, project management, and other disciplines that are critical to a CIO's success. Consulting experience often gives a CIO a client-focused orientation and the ability to grasp business models and concepts quickly. Too much consulting experience, however, can lead to an inability to lead teams and development.

—*Martha Heller, Heller Search Associates*

- Low. Consulting experience generally detracts from institutional problem-solving experience, based on the simple fact that consultants don't generally stay for the long-term grunt work of implementation.

—*Derek Wilkinson, Boyden Global Executive Search*

- Medium.

—*Beverly Lieberman, Halbrecht Lieberman Associates*

- Medium. Consulting experience is valuable and gives CIOs a platform to learn the foundation skills of problem solving, communication, and program or project management. Those with consulting experience tend to stand out as leaders who think more holistically and see the big picture.

—*Kathryn Graham Shannon, Heidrick & Stuggles*

The responses to this question provide very valuable insights, from my perspective. While I do believe that CIOs need to have consulting experience, I agree with the team comments that too much is overkill and that during the interview, CIOs need to stress the business benefits of a previous consulting engagement rather than just talk about what and how the engagement proceeded. I do feel strongly that those who do not have consulting experience will probably not be as savvy in managing consultants and outsourced vendors. Getting the experience from the inside is invaluable.

What other ways can first-time CIO candidates differentiate themselves from others, and how important is it to do that on their resumes rather than in the interview process?

- First-time CIO candidates can differentiate themselves by having worked in a part of the business that is not IT, such as sales, operations, or marketing. Having experience presenting to the board of directors, having built great relationships with key members of the business, and having stepped up to take a leadership role in an enterprise initiative that is not necessarily an IT initiative is a way to differentiate.
—*Martha Heller, Heller Search Associates*

- On the resume, use a tone of "business partner" as opposed to "technologist." You'll have plenty of time to show how technically savvy you are. In the interview process, ask questions. Demonstrate how you probe to understand how to devise solutions that are short-term, medium, and long-term. Don't just let the questions you are asked define their [the interviewers'] understanding of you.
—*Derek Wilkinson, Boyden Global Executive Search*

- The resume should reflect accomplishments of note that contribute to top-line sales or cost reduction and management. The resume needs to be appealing to a CEO or a CFO and not be simply a CIO job description. It needs to point out key achievements that are meaningful to business leaders.
—*Beverly Lieberman, Halbrecht Lieberman Associates*

(Continued)

EXECUTIVE RECRUITER SURVEY (*Continued*)

- It's very important for first-time CIO candidates to differentiate themselves. One way of differentiating yourself from the pack is to focus on the customer and what is right for the customer. This will help align technology with business goals and keep the IT organization focused on delivering added value. There are far too many CIOs who lose sight of the endgame (the ultimate customer) and therefore aren't able to deliver success, in the eyes of the business they serve.
—*Kathryn Graham Shannon, Heidrick & Stuggles*

What are the three most important things that CIO candidates should highlight during the interview process to executive recruiters and potential employers?

- Team leadership: the ability to bring IT together with the business.
- Execution: the ability to complete multiple projects on time and on budget.
- Strategic thinking: the ability to provide the business with solutions rather than just taking the order.
—*Martha Heller, Heller Search Associates*

- Agility.
- Team approach.
- Solutions orientation.
—*Derek Wilkinson, Boyden Global Executive Search*

- Examples of leadership.
- The ability to deliver on promises.
- The ability to add value.
—*Beverly Lieberman, Halbrecht Lieberman Associates*

- Progression and effect brought to the company one has served in and clearly articulated (personal and team) achievements as they relate to the overall business strategy or big picture.
- Strengths and weaknesses.

- A defined leadership strategy.

—*Kathryn Graham Shannon, Heidrick & Stuggles*

How important are financial management skills in becoming a CIO, and why?

- High. IT is typically the largest budget in the company, and IT investments are a critical element in a company's growth. The CIO has to be able to understand the financial implications of IT investment decisions.

—*Martha Heller, Heller Search Associates*

- High. IT can be one of the largest costs to any organization, and being able to demonstrate fiscal responsibility and budget management is not just nice to have, it is a necessity.

—*Derek Wilkinson, Boyden Global Executive Search*

- Low. CIOs have to work with budgets and negotiate with vendors on a routine basis. They need to understand the cost of IT delivery.

—*Beverly Lieberman, Halbrecht Lieberman Associates*

- High. Very important. IT should run like a business, and having financial management skills is important for any business leader.

—*Kathryn Graham Shannon, Heidrick & Stuggles*

I'm in the camp of high importance, myself. As stated by several of the recruiting experts, IT is usually a substantial percentage of an institution's budget—operating and capital. Without solid financial skills, a CIO may very well end up reporting to the CFO. CIOs must know the investment effects of their investments, including capitalizing a purchase and depreciating it versus outsourcing a solution to a cloud provider and spending operating dollars.

What is the best academic background for the CIO role today, and why?

- The best combination is a bachelor of science degree in computer science and a master's in business administration (MBA). While the ability to write code is not on the list of CIO skills, technical acumen

(Continued)

EXECUTIVE RECRUITER SURVEY (*Continued*)

is. A solid foundation in computer science gives the CIO the ability to understand systems development and architecture and to make the right IT investment decisions. An MBA gives the CIO many of the other important skills, like business acumen. The CIO of a very large company would be less in need of a technical background than the CIO of a small company.

—*Martha Heller, Heller Search Associates*

- I don't think one academic background or another really matters, but the education beyond IT is something that shows how well-rounded one is.

—*Derek Wilkinson, Boyden Global Executive Search*

- An MBA to prepare for the business aspects of the job.

—*Beverly Lieberman, Halbrecht Lieberman Associates*

- Computer science, all types of engineering, or a mathematics undergraduate degree. Plus an MBA.

—*Kathryn Graham Shannon, Heidrick & Stuggles*

I actually have a strong recommendation on this question. I believe that a great candidate will have the foundation of a technical undergraduate degree (computer science, math, or software engineering) plus an MBA. I run into far too many nontechnical CIOs who simply do not understand the complexities of modern technical software and hardware solutions. The ones I meet who are solid are role models, are confident, and don't have to rely on their subordinates for a decision that if made incorrectly could affect their careers.

What is the minimum number of years of work experience that is necessary to be a viable candidate for a CIO role today?

- There are exceptions, but I would expect that viable first-time CIO candidates would need to be in their 30s, so 12 years' experience at the very minimum.

—*Martha Heller, Heller Search Associates*

- 12–15 years.
—*Derek Wilkinson, Boyden Global Executive Search*

- 15 years.
—*Beverly Lieberman, Halbrecht Lieberman Associates*

- There is no minimum in terms of years of experience. I just placed a very successful CIO who has less than 10 years of experience. He is incredibly smart, detail oriented, and business savvy; communicates succinctly; and has a high degree of technical knowledge.
—*Kathryn Graham Shannon, Heidrick & Stuggles*

What career advice would you give to midlevel professionals today to help them prepare for a CIO role in the future?

- Find two mentors—one a seasoned CIO and the other a "business" executive—and work with them regularly.

- Get very good at building relationships with your peers in all parts of the company. IT strategies are won or lost on the strength of the CIO's relationship with his or her business peers.

- Know your strengths and choose your employment opportunities based on them. Are you a wonderful operations leader but not a strategic thinker? Then either go for an operationally oriented CIO job or be sure to hire a great strategist as part of your senior leadership team.
—*Martha Heller, Heller Search Associates*

- Build relationships with those you serve in the operations of the organization.
—*Derek Wilkinson, Boyden Global Executive Search*

- Get an MBA and work on customer facing systems. Be current with outsourcing, cloud computing, SaaS, IaaS, and PaaS. Consider an international assignment.
—*Beverly Lieberman, Halbrecht Lieberman Associates*

(Continued)

EXECUTIVE RECRUITER SURVEY (*Continued*)

- Do what is right for the business first. Invest in relationship building, people development, and communication skills. Get out of
your office and walk the halls—get to know your team and the
teams you serve. Run IT like a business. Stay current and think strategically about where things are going.

—*Kathryn Graham Shannon, Heidrick & Stuggles*

What percentage of CIOs are hired from within their existing companies?

- From anecdotal experience, I would say less than 20 percent.

—*Martha Heller, Heller Search Associates*

- 50 percent.

—*Derek Wilkinson, Boyden Global Executive Search*

- 25 percent.

—*Beverly Lieberman, Halbrecht Lieberman Associates*

- Approximately 50 percent.

—*Kathryn Graham Shannon, Heidrick & Stuggles*

**What new skills are required for today's CIOs compared to the skills that were
required five to seven years ago? Thus, what has changed?**

- The ability to innovate.

- The ability to meet with external customers.

- Global leadership.

- Data strategy, data management, and business intelligence.

—*Martha Heller, Heller Search Associates*

- Not much has changed, in my opinion. The technology always
changes, but understanding how to make things work well is based
on old-fashioned good sense, project management ability, leadership, and vision.

—*Derek Wilkinson, Boyden Global Executive Search*

- The range of technologies includes mobile technology, social networking, business analytics, and cloud computing. I don't think we were focused on these five to seven years ago.

—*Beverly Lieberman, Halbrecht Lieberman Associates*

- The CIO is asked to deliver value-added IT. With the consumerization of technology, businesses are being forced to rethink and revise their processes to respond to current ways of conducting business (e.g., digital, data, mobile, security). Technology is moving so quickly, and it's difficult to get in front of the consumer or customer. Businesses need to respond quickly but also have agility.

—*Kathryn Graham Shannon, Heidrick & Stuggles*

I couldn't agree more with this panel on these answers. Mobile, social, and cloud computing are driving change, followed by figuring out what to do with all the data and how to secure the data.

What is the most common next step for sitting CIOs who want to expand out of IT?

- First is what I call the "CIO and" phenomenon, when a CIO takes on an additional title, such as vice president of strategic planning or vice president of customer care. Once he or she has proven him- or herself in that dual role, the next step is to COO.

—*Martha Heller, Heller Search Associates*

- A COO or another operations role, although finance is on the rise. My rationale is that the good CIOs have invested themselves in those functions.

—*Derek Wilkinson, Boyden Global Executive Search*

- The COO or CEO of a technology-related company.

—*Beverly Lieberman, Halbrecht Lieberman Associates*

- The CEO or COO.

—*Kathryn Graham Shannon, Heidrick & Stuggles*

(Continued)

EXECUTIVE RECRUITER SURVEY (*Continued*)

What are the necessary skills for CIOs who are looking to take the next step?

- Leadership.
- Six Sigma, Lean, or some other kind of continuous improvement methodology.
- Relationships.
- The ability to shake off the technology-solution view of every problem.
- Business acumen.

—*Martha Heller, Heller Search Associates*

- Demonstrated visionary leadership.

—*Derek Wilkinson, Boyden Global Executive Search*

- The ability to run IT as a business, make customers happy, and manage costs to ensure profitability.

—*Beverly Lieberman, Halbrecht Lieberman Associates*

The insights and recommendations from this talented group of executive recruiting professionals is amazing, and I hope it has been very helpful to aspiring CIOs and to CIOs looking for the next challenge. I hope a lot of readers break out their highlighting pens. There are lots of pearls of wisdom in this chapter, and it's from the folks who are paid very well to find top IT talent.

Tomorrow's Leadership Skills

Technology management is certainly changing. The experience, demonstrated results, and skills required by today's CIOs are as demanding as any time in modern history and throughout the evolution of the role itself. In a recent *CIO* magazine article, Martha Heller noted the skills that will be required by CIOs in the future. Heller, president of the executive recruiting firm Heller Search Associates, is a frequent contributor to *CIO* magazine, a seasoned executive recruiting professional, a friend and key member of my network, and one of the distinguished executive recruiters contributing to this book. According to Heller's research, CIOs will need the following skills in the near future:

- Vendor management experience.
- IT governance knowledge.
- Financial expertise. As cloud computing adoption increases, CIOs need to be able to understand the ROI of technology and how that affects amortization schedules.
- Team leadership skills. This includes the humility to be able to hire and surround yourself with people who are smarter than you are.
- Experience with corporate ups and downs. Include acquisitions and divestitures to the list of experiences needed.
- Exposure to external customers.
- A proven ability to innovate.
- Consulting experience.
- Experience running a profit-loss business unit. This will most likely be a growing trend for future CIOs, but it is one set of skills and experience to prepare for, if you can find the opportunity.
- Industry and geographical diversity. This builds a well-seasoned executive who can adapt to a changing landscape or culture.
- Talent supply chain management. Partner with colleges and universities to better prepare the next generation of IT leaders.[5]

What Did I Do to Prepare?

I've had great success to date in working with executive recruiting firms. They are an important aspect of my current success and are anticipated to play a large role in the remainder of my career. Make contact and build relationships that are long-lasting and valuable to both parties. As advised by the seasoned recruiting teams, I have continued learning. The application of IT that matters most is solving a business problem with the right technical solutions and speaking about the accomplishments in business terms, not IT-speak. I have to force myself time and time again to speak technically to the IT team, strategically to the CEO, and in business terms to other business executives, as appropriate for the department or specialty.

The IT professionals who rise today are the ones who learn the business, speak the business language, and solve problems through technology in the most cost-efficient manner possible.

Recommendations

To close this chapter, I advise sitting CIOs and professionals aspiring to become CIOs not to lose focus on building the right resume of accomplishments and increasing levels of responsibility that may lead to running a world-class IT organization. The following recommendations are designed to help candidates prepare for working with a reputable executive recruiting firm to land their next challenges:

- Speak in the right terms to the right people. IT folks have a tendency to speak in IT acronyms too often, especially around other business professionals. Know your audience and speak to them in *their* language. Communicate these skills to your recruiter. They are the first test before your first company interview.
- Make contact with key recruiting firms (local, regional, then progress to national and international) and build relationships that are long-lasting and valuable to both parties. Bill yourself as valuable to them. Remember, they make money from candidates.
- Make an effort to write about projects and/or IT strategies that have produced business results. Publishing articles is an excellent way to raise your profile and get noticed. It's also how conference coordinators look for speaking talent. The two skills, writing and speaking, go hand in hand; they can greatly improve your exposure and catch the eye of an executive recruiting professional. It's actually how I met Martha Heller more than a dozen years ago.
- Expand your network and focus on non-IT parties who can better link you to business contacts at other organizations.
- Find a mentor if you are a midlevel professional and ask him or her to help guide your career. Don't make the relationship one-way (receiving). Feed it.
- If you're a sitting CIO, become a mentor. Pay it forward and help raise the next generation of IT leaders.
- Get some international experience, if possible. Large consulting firms offer an excellent opportunity to gain great experience with international clients. The experience also helps candidates to learn about different cultures and environments.
- Focus on accomplishments and try IT best practices that solve business-related problems and can be measured and perceived by your customers.
- Consider getting an MBA to complement your undergraduate degree and your experience. CIOs who have MBAs are on a more even footing with other executives, who usually have MBAs as well. Be wary

of for-profit online programs that are costly and may not compete with traditional nonprofit academic institutions. Consult some of the plethora of research on the differences between for-profit and non-profit educational institutions and the value they bring to the student before you apply and attend. Get into the most reputable school you can afford. The reputation of the academic institution matters.

- Last, but certainly not least, build your brand. Your brand is more than just a job history with titles on LinkedIn. It's about what you've accomplished, what you've written, conferences you've attended and presentations you've given, and your expertise. Your branded site should communicate to the readers, including executive recruiters, what you're capable of doing in the future and a little about your character by how you write about accomplishments.

Notes

1. Dwight D. Eisenhower, Inspirational Quotes, www.inspirational-quotes.info/leadership.html (accessed July 18, 2012).
2. Elaine Pofeldt, "Get Noticed and Promoted," CNNMoney, July 16, 2012, money.cnn .com/2012/07/16/pf/job-promotion.moneymag/index.htm (accessed July 16, 2012).
3. Chad Brooks, "What Is LinkedIn?" *Business News Daily*, May 9, 2012, www.businessnewsdaily .com/2489-linkedin.html (accessed November 1, 2012).
4. Gerry McCartney, Leading Gen Y," *CIO*, May 1, 2009, p. 54.
5. Martha Heller, "Tomorrow's Leadership Skills," *CIO*, June 1, 2012, p. 43.

CHAPTER 7

Cloud Computing Strategies and Risks

Try not to become a man of success, but a man of value.

—ALBERT EINSTEIN[1]

Cloud computing is no longer a myth but a reality. CIOs from all around the world are transferring certain functions of their IT organizations into the cloud. Those who are extremely security conscious keep their most treasured technology and data behind the firewalls in their data centers. Risk-aware CIOs leverage a combination of private and public cloud technologies. SaaS vendors and applications are a large force behind the growth of cloud technology today. The time it takes to turn on a major application in the cloud can be many months (and sometimes years), days, or a few months.

Cloud computing is here today. Our business customers are demanding that we engage in order to meet more timely demands for IT systems and services. This chapter provides a road map for today's IT professionals and executives interested in leveraging this great resource.

A Cloud Computing Overview

Let me be clear: IT has been utilizing computing services in a variety of ways for years—well before the concept was branded as cloud computing. Managed hosting services, application service providers (ASPs), and SaaS have offered organizations computing infrastructure and software services for years, outside their core internal computing capabilities and data centers. I offer the following definitions of IT acronyms to clarify exactly what cloud computing is today in the market:

- **Cloud computing.** This is "a computing capability that provides an abstraction between the computing resources and its underlying technology architecture (e.g. servers, storage, and networks), enabling convenient, on-demand network access to a shared pool of configurable computing resources that can be rapidly provisioned and released with minimal management effort or service provider interaction."[2]

  My definition of cloud computing can be boiled down to something as simple as this: infrastructure, network, security (shared or dedicated), and software services available outside an organization's core data centers, control, and management—accessible over the public Internet or via private dedicated circuits or virtual private networks.

- **IaaS.** Infrastructure as a service is the delivery of computing infrastructure (storage, hardware, servers, networking), typically virtualized, as a service for use.[3] Examples of IaaS include the Amazon Elastic Compute Cloud Web Service (EC2) and Simple Storage Services (S3) product services that offer computing resources for use through a billing model that charges by use, scale, and duration of time. IaaS is rapidly moving into other types of infrastructure that expand beyond traditional servers, disks, networks, and security. Phone infrastructure solutions are now available on the market so that customers can move their phone system and infrastructure *outside* their data center and access that IaaS and SaaS over the public Internet or via private dedicated circuits. Leading Internet phone companies include Cisco and M5.

- **PaaS.** Platform as a service is closely related to IaaS, in which organizations rent hardware, operating systems, and storage and network capacity over the Internet. PaaS has several advantages for developers, including the frequent configuration and upgrading of operating systems for diverse sources that cross geographical boundaries.[4]

- **SaaS.** Software as a service contains cloud *application* services over the Internet. SaaS was previously defined as an ASP. Examples of application SaaS solutions are Salesforce's CRM, Marketing Cloud, and Service Cloud applications; Google's Gmail and apps; Microsoft Dynamics, Microsoft Exchange; and Oracle's On-Demand application suite of software, delivered over the Internet. In this model, customers need not purchase any server, application, or other infrastructure needed to run the application other than the license to use the product, typically by a named or concurrent user.

  Great SaaS companies are architected and built from the ground up so organizations can interface with their systems and data via Web services and application programming interfaces (APIs), which allows the customers to integrate information between applications regardless of whether they are in the cloud (public or private) or on-premise (behind their firewalls and inside their managed data centers). Salesforce is a perfect example of a company that has built its product for integration. I'll discuss integration later in this chapter; it requires a more complete explanation and a set of recommendations for the readers.

- **Cloud provider.** This is any vendor that provides cloud-based platforms, infrastructure, applications, or storage as a fee-based service.[5]
- **Elastic cloud computing.** This is the ability to quickly and dynamically provision and deprovision infrastructure—including the performance management of the central processing unit (CPU), memory, and disk tiers—to meet demands for peak usage.[6] This elastic ability allows organizations to quickly burst resources in advance of known computing needs, such as those associated with a Web or social media campaign or a public relations effort that may draw significant users to the Web-based computing resources that are branded with the corporate name.
- **Private cloud.** A private cloud typically includes infrastructure, storage, network (PaaS and IaaS) and applications (SaaS) that are an extension of your corporate network (i.e., behind the firewall).[7] Private cloud infrastructure and applications can be inside your firewall and managed by an outside vendor or, more commonly, sitting inside a vendor's data center but carved out away from other customers and linked to the corporate network as an extension of that network behind the company's firewall. IBM and Rackspace are two good vendor examples who provide these services.
- **Public cloud.** This is a vendor landscape that offers some form of infrastructure, storage, network, and applications accessible over the public Internet.[8] Examples of public cloud vendors include Amazon, Salesforce, Blackbaud, Sugar CRM, Google, Microsoft, and Rackspace—all are accessible only through the public Internet and most likely on a shared infrastructure (server, disk, and network) that's easily provisioned to add new customers. Public cloud vendors offering SaaS solutions contain the underlying database management systems that house a customer's data and information. Some vendors are designed to store this information in shared databases, while others use separate database instances or containers for each customer. I highly recommend asking how your information will be stored before committing to a public cloud or SaaS solution.
- **Hybrid cloud.** This is a combination of public cloud and private cloud services.

I firmly believe that the hybrid cloud will be the most common use for organizations today, given the flexibility of placing their important corporate data and information either outside the firewall or behind it. The classic reasoning behind the hybrid cloud option is that it gives CIOs the most flexibility in deciding where to put their systems, data, and applications and how far to move them outside their control, especially for security purposes. Organizations need to determine the risk level before deciding to jump to the cloud and determine whether they should play in the full public cloud space or opt for a more secure (and controlled and connected) network associated with a private cloud offering. My advice regarding the use of public or private clouds or on-premise solutions for CIOs and CISOs today is as follows:

- Push the systems and data into the public cloud whenever you have the least concerns about the security of that information. Ensure that the roles and profiles associated with the SaaS solutions sitting in the public cloud are rock solid and as tight as they can be. If you want a little more comfort regarding security, ensure that your applications can be accessed from only one of your corporate offices via Internet provider ranging services offered by many of the SaaS vendors. That guarantees that you can implement data loss prevention (DLP) software when you can ensure that the assets that are using cloud services are coming from computing platforms that you control (and can ensure are being monitored by DLP software) and manage.
- Opt for a private cloud offering for systems and data that need to be very tightly controlled and secure, and link your corporate data center to the vendor's data center via dedicated circuits or virtual private networks to ensure security.

If you're really concerned about the most sensitive data and systems, keep them in-house and on-premise in your data centers. That said, and knowing that most risk of data loss and theft comes from the inside, I believe strongly in the new era of DLP software in order to know how your information and data are being treated, handled, and transmitted. With the clear trend to public, private, and hybrid cloud computing and the decentralization of an organization's data and systems, DLP will become an increasingly important tool for protecting an organization's key data assets.

How to Prepare for the Cloud

Before an organization takes a leap into the cloud, it should look at several criteria:

- What is the organization's risk profile—high, medium, or low? The answer to this question alone may determine the leap to the cloud or the desire to control more of your applications in-house or at least through private cloud solutions.

- Are your data centers and corporate offices optimized for the cloud? You'll need network redundancy, lots of bandwidth, and potentially (WAN) acceleration services and increased security.
- Transform the desktop and mobile environments to empower the users.
- Determine which applications should be moved to the cloud and define your portfolio of on-premise, private cloud, and public cloud resources and vendors. There should be a business value and benefit to moving certain functions or applications into the cloud. Identify the criteria; look at the benefits and risks *before* committing to a cloud trend. Consider keeping non-Web-based applications that may be legacy client-server applications on-premise instead of putting terminal services capabilities into your cloud vendor.
- Determine the security and monitoring (based on your risk profile) that is needed to move into the cloud.
- Develop and/or refine your SLAs to include variations of the current offerings as a result of conforming to external vendors and *their* SLAs, terms, and conditions.
- Industrialize IT operations to improve productivity, monitor performance, and manage internal and cloud services.[9]

Forrester Research conducted a survey of IT infrastructure and operations leaders to determine their top challenges in the months ahead (see Exhibit 7.1). The top three priorities included the effective and secure use of cloud computing,

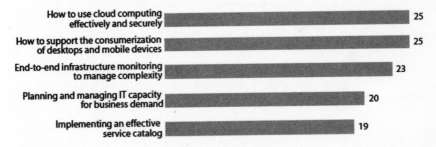

"Select five of the top challenges you will face over the next six months."

How to use cloud computing effectively and securely	25
How to support the consumerization of desktops and mobile devices	25
End-to-end infrastructure monitoring to manage complexity	23
Planning and managing IT capacity for business demand	20
Implementing an effective service catalog	19

Base: 36 infrastructure and Operations executives from Forrester's Infrastructure & Operations Council (multiple responses accepted)

Source: 2011 Q2 Global Infrastructure And Operations Council Challenge Assessment Online Survey

Exhibit 7.1   The Top Priorities of IT Infrastructure and Operations Leadership
Source: Forrester Research, Inc.

the support of consumer devices (including mobile), and planning and managing business demand, either via internal or cloud-based services.[10]

Planning for the Cloud: How One Vendor Does It Well

A prominent cloud vendor, Rackspace, has some really solid planning steps and services to help companies move to their cloud offerings, both public and private.

Rackspace outlines the following steps for the movement or use of public cloud services:

- Planning includes decisions on cloud servers, sites, storage, platform, networking, monitoring, backup, and performance. The vendor offers advice on capacity planning, scale, security, server configuration, and selection of application or Web servers (e.g., Apache, IIS).
- Installation includes the provisioning of servers, databases, patch management, database installation, configuration, security and firewalls, load balancing, and e-mail integration and relays for your environment.
- Configuration typically includes operating system configuration, database optimization, domain management in and out of the cloud environment, Web and app server configuration, and load balancing configuration.
- Patch management.
- Backup strategy and management.
- Monitoring and threshold alerts.
- Troubleshooting.[11]

There are lots of IaaS, PaaS, and SaaS cloud vendors on the market offering infrastructure and applications—most with no software or hardware required on the customer side (beyond application integration). Organizations contemplating moving or expanding into the cloud should do lots of research on vendors, solutions, costs, and approaches for cloud computing. I highly recommend the use and services of IT advisory firms like Forrester, Gartner, and IDC to assist in any analysis, migration, and management of your cloud portfolio.

The Benefits and Effects of Cloud Computing

The leap to cloud computing has the following benefits and effects on an IT department and the organization it supports or serves:

- Organizations can provision servers, disk systems, and applications much faster than internally managed and maintained systems. Some vendors offer minutes versus hours or days to bring online computing services. Amazon is a leader in this with its EC2 cloud offering.

■ Cost savings. Cloud allows its customers to pay for what they use. Companies therefore pay only for the computing and application services that they use. If they decrease or scale down performance during off-peak periods, their costs go down.

■ Elastic computing options in most cloud vendor solutions (IaaS, PaaS) allow companies to increase or decrease system scale and performance as needed and pay only for what and when they use those services. This differs entirely from the utilization model associated with systems *inside* the corporate data center, where system utilization is lower but can be optimized through virtualization technologies. Virtualizing systems allows CIOs and infrastructure managers to better utilize their infrastructure by managing the number of virtual servers (virtual machines for VMWare) to a physical server to ensure their getting the best utilization for their investment. Regardless of the level of utilization inside the corporate data center, the organization has already purchased all of the computing power and infrastructure, most likely through a capital IT purchase. Elastic cloud computing moves away from a total investment for unused assets and lets customers pay only for what they use.

■ The effect of purchasing cloud services is that they are operating expenses, not traditional capital expenses. This means that a higher portion of IT expenses will occur during the current year and potentially decrease net income (depending on the size and revenue of the organization) as a result of 100 percent of the expenses occurring in the current year, versus only a portion with capitalization and depreciation. Depreciating IT infrastructure and large software applications typically results in costs being spread out over a series of years through depreciation (typically three to five years). As a result, a large capital purchase may occur in the current year's financial expenses at only 20 to 33 percent of the purchase cost in a capitalization model. CIOs need to adjust their budgets accordingly to include more operating spending and less capital spending if they are moving or accelerating to the cloud.

■ Cloud storage is cheaper than purchasing and maintaining large internal SAN systems. Forrester Research conducted a super analysis comparing 100 terabytes of internal and cloud storage and found that the cost to deploy and maintain 100 terabytes of storage internally is approximately $1 million, compared to a fraction of that—$250,000—with a cloud offering.[12] Exhibits 7.2 and 7.3, respectively, depict the underlying costs associated with internal and cloud storage associated with 100 terabytes of space.

Internal storage

	Assumptions	Calculations	
TB of actual data	100	$400,000	Acquisition cost of base amount of storage
Years expected lifespan of storage	4	300	Usable TB required including data copies
$/usable GB purchase price	$4	420	Total usable TB required for primary, copies, and utilization
Copies of data for redundancy	3	$1,680,000	Acquisition cost of total storage requirement
Typical utilization of storage (excluding RAID and system resource overhead)	60%	$420,000	Annualized storage acquisition cost based on lifespan
Typical TB/FTE	150	2.8	FTE requirement for storage admin of stated TB count
Fully loaded $/FTE	$120,000	$336,000	Annual storage admin cost
Facilities and power charge (of storage acquisition cost)	5%	$84,000	Annual facilities and power charge
Years of included warranty	3	$63,000	Annualized maintenance charge
Percent of original purchase price for additional warranty years	15%	$52,500	Annualized data migration charge
Cost per usable TB data migration	$500	$955,500	Total annual cost of internal storage

Exhibit 7.2   Traditional File Storage Systems Are Expensive to Buy and Run
Source: Forrester Research, Inc.

- The cloud touts better monitoring and potentially improved security as new security services are deployed to the cloud. This is still up in the air from my perspective, but I'll discuss security in more detail later in this chapter. Hardware and monitoring services have become commodities, since they are now plentifully available from a variety of cloud vendors. Instead of spending time on purchasing, installing, maintaining, and monitoring IT core server and disk infrastructure, consider pushing some of it to the cloud. The trick is *when*. For organizations that have recently made significant purchases of servers and disk systems (SANs), I recommend focusing on cloud applications before infrastructure cloud services. Doing so will allow the organization to depreciate much of the expense associated with acquiring hardware. When the hardware and infrastructure purchases get closer to the end of their depreciation schedules, that's the time to consider IaaS and PaaS expansion—when they are nearly or fully depreciated. The CFO will love you for this type of creative financial thinking and planning.
- The cloud offers exposure to a myriad of applications that CIOs can quickly turn up and provide to their organizations. Examples of quick deployment of certain applications include CRM, e-mail, collaboration,

Cloud storage

	Assumptions		Calculations	
TB of actual data	100		$11,800	Monthly cost of cloud storage
$/GB/month cloud charge	$0.118		$141,600	Annual cost of cloud storage
Months/year	12		$10,000	Total data-transfer-in charges
GB/TB	1,000		50	TB out/month
$/GB data-transfer-in rate	$0.1		$90,000	Annual data-transfer-out charges
Initial data in, assumed in annual cost	100%		$0	Additional redundancy capacity charges
$/GB data-transfer-out rate (simplified)	$0.15		$0	Cloud gateway annualized charge
Data out/month	50%		$20,000	Incremental annual network charge
Included copies of data for redundancy	3		$251,600	Total annual cost of cloud storage
Cloud gateway hardware/software charge	$0			
Years expected lifespan of gateway	4			
Incremental annual network charge	20,000			

Exhibit 7.3   Cloud Storage Is More Straightforward and a Lot Cheaper Than Traditional Storage
Source: Forrester Research, Inc.

financial management, phones, business intelligence, file storage, and a lot of application-specific markets and products—all deployable faster in the cloud than internally.

- The cloud offers reduced reliance on maintenance or patching and instead allows an IT organization to focus on implementing services and applications that serve it—and doing so more nimbly and rapidly.
- Cloud computing vendors typically handle most of the monitoring of services. This can relieve IT departments of another tedious role that's provided within the network services and operations department subunit of IT.
- Cloud offerings, especially SaaS, offer built-in disaster recovery business continuity (DRBC) capabilities and can greatly simply a CIO's DR strategy, investment, and commitment to testing. When an organization commits to a solution like Salesforce's CRM application, DRBC becomes Salesforce's problem, not the problem of the IT department of the customer. That's a huge weight off the CIO and can be a great reduction of time and effort associated with putting in place the appropriate IT insurance policy to hedge against natural and man-made system failures.

Forrester Research predicts the following about the cloud:

- Highly empowered resourceful operatives (HEROs, typically in the business unit) will use new cloud tools and applications to optimize their jobs. They will focus more on functionality and less on integration and security.
- Internal IT cloud efforts are likely to fail. Forrester considers full implementation to include workload automation, self-service portals, and cost accounting, not just the cloudwashing of virtualized environments. According to Forrester's 2011 prediction, the jury is still out on this one.
- The rush to IaaS will not gain in traction, as previously thought, to implement a private cloud environment. Organizations will attempt to keep some of their infrastructure services inside while more often exploring the cloud for application offerings.
- Community clouds may materialize for empowered vertical markets (like financial services, education, or the public sector). At this time, Forrester's original prediction of community clouds coming to full fruition is still to be determined.
- Workstation applications will bring high-performance computing (HPC) to the masses. Autodesk and Adobe have made strides in this market, but the completeness of this prediction still remains to be seen.
- Cloud analytics lets leaders break away from the pack. Real-time analytics, social media analysis, and gleaning business value from unstructured data will give organizations a competitive advantage if they can use business intelligence and analytics better and faster than their competitors do.
- Cloud may transform your information into a profit center. Amazon, Microsoft, and Google are laying foundations for commercializing corporate data. Whether this prediction fully comes to pass will be based on how comfortably and quickly organizations let their corporate data be made available for these services.
- Cloud standards will continue to evolve. Forrester has not released a prediction date for when standards will be clear and adopted.
- Cloud economics will reach new heights, going beyond the basics of cloud economics and moving toward optimizing application configurations and designs to maximize the benefits of pay-per-use pricing.
- Cloud security will be proved, but not by providers alone. Recently, leading cloud vendors have gotten serious about security and earned key certifications (ISO 27001, 20001, PCI-DSS, and FISMA). In the future, enterprises will take a larger role in securing their use of clouds and the information contained within them. I believe DLP will be

a key component, along with better cloud security certification and training coming online in the near future.[13]

Growth Trends and Costs ✳

The costs for cloud services vary, depending on what you're buying: infrastructure, platform, network, database, or application. I'll highlight a few services and their pricing models to illustrate the differences.

Growth Trends

The following are some of the statistics (restated from Chapter 2) that support the adoption and innovative use of cloud computing:

- One billion monthly active users accessed Facebook's web site at the end of September 2012, with 81 percent of them outside the United States and Canada.[14]
- Twitter, a communications tool that's funded primarily by advertising, experienced an average of 140 million tweets per day in 2011, up from 40 million per day in 2010.[15]
- The global private cloud market was $7.81 billion in 2011. It's predicted to reach $15.93 billion by 2015.[16]
- The SaaS market represents the largest portion of the global cloud market, at $21.2 billion in total revenue in 2011.[17]

Costs

Costs for the cloud vary, depending on vendor, service, software application, and support. Below is a sampling of some cloud fees.

Amazon Public Cloud—EC2

Amazon supports a variety of operating systems (e.g., Redhat Linux, Windows Server, openSuSE Linux, OpenSolaris, Cent OS, and Oracle Linux) on a variety of platform options. The company gives customers an easy way to purchase and provision premade environments depending on their needs. They have recently introduced a free tier of pricing to entice new users to their offerings. Server offerings are priced in on-demand instances and reserved instances.[18] On-demand allows customers complete flexibility to set up, use, and decommission services when they need them and pay only for the time they use those services (charged by the hour) without any long-term commitments. Exhibit 7.4 highlights a sampling of hourly pricing (variable by Linux

Exhibit 7.4   Amazon On-Demand Instance Pricing

Standard On-Demand Instances	Linux or Unix	Windows
Small	$0.080 per hour	$0.115 per hour
Medium	$0.160 per hour	$0.230 per hour
Large	$0.320 per hour	$0.460 per hour
Extra-large	$0.640 per hour	$0.920 per hour[19]

and Windows) for a variety of computing instances and servers published on the Amazon EC2 site for on-demand instances.

Exhibit 7.5 highlights the savings customers can achieve by leveraging reserved instances and committing to longer periods or contracts. As a result, an extra-large server in a reserved instance can cost a customer $3,022.88 per year in operating lease fees.

Exhibit 7.5   Amazon Reserved Instance Pricing

Standard Reserved Instances	Upfront	1-Year Term Hourly	Upfront	3-Year Term Hourly
Small	$ 69	$0.039 per hour	$106.30	$0.031 per hour
Medium	$138	$0.078 per hour	$212.50	$0.063 per hour
Large	$276	$0.156 per hour	$425.20	$0.124 per hour
Extra-large	$552	$0.312 per hour	$850.40	$0.248 per hour[20]

Rackspace Cloud Costs

Rackspace, another leading cloud vendor that plays very strongly in the IaaS and PaaS market, offers a variety of cloud services, priced individually by the specific service offered: Cloud Servers, Sites, Databases, Backup, Monitoring, Load Balancers, Files, DNS, and so on. Exhibit 7.6 highlights some of the server-based pricing that depends on memory, operating system, and the use of a database management system. The fees are very reasonable, as noted for a Windows server with 15 gigabytes of memory and a database server for $1.90 per hour ($1,387 per month). [21]

Exhibit 7.6   Rackspace Cloud Server Pricing

Memory	Linux	Windows	Windows + SQL Web	Windows + SQL Standard
1GB	$0.06 per hour	$0.08 per hour		
2GB	$0.12 per hour	$0.16 per hour	$0.22 per hour	$0.88 per hour
8GB	$0.48 per hour	$0.58 per hour	$0.64 per hour	$1.30 per hour
15GB	$0.90 per hour	$1.08 per hour	$1.14 per hour	$2.63 per hour[22]

What's clear to me is that the cost of cloud services can add up, and if cloud services are not utilized around the clock, they may not be the best investment for a company. A database server at Rackspace for $1,387 per month or $16,644 per year may or may not be the best use of a company's IT investment when capitalization and other total costs of ownership associated with managing the asset are considered. My advice to IT managers and others on evaluating cloud services is this: Do your homework on the services and costs before determining to use cloud IaaS or PaaS versus internally managed services. For some organizations with little capital to spend, cloud may be just the right thing. For larger organizations, I believe it requires a thorough cost analysis and ROI calculation before going all-in.

SaaS Application Costs

SaaS solutions are commonly priced by a named or concurrent user. The monthly fees typically include the cost of the license, any infrastructure (e.g., server, network, security, or support) necessary to provide the application to the customer over the public Internet. As a result, SaaS vendors include many components of PaaS and IaaS associated with their software offerings as part of their pricing. Salesforce's CRM is one of the most highly rated and used CRM systems in the world. Salesforce is an example of a quickly growing company. The following are some recent statistics associated with Salesforce:

- The company's customer base grew from 63,000 in 2009 to more than 100,000 in 2012.
- The applications available for use with the Salesforce product available on its AppExchange grew from 1,000 applications in 2010 to 1,500 in August 2012.
- As of September 26, 2012, more than 1.4 million applications were downloaded and installed from the AppExchange.[23]

Salesforce prices its CRM software by named user. Exhibit 7.7 provides per user pricing for a variety of license models, from small groups to large enterprises. For a full unlimited license with premier support and use of the social collaboration application called Chatter, it would cost an organization of 1,000 CRM users $250 per month of IT operating expenses per user, or $250,000 per month, or $3 million per year at list pricing.[24]

Exhibit 7.7 Salesforce Sales Cloud CRM Pricing

Contact Manager	Group	Professional	Enterprise	Unlimited
$5 per user per month	$15 per user per month	$65 per user per month	$125 per user per month	$250 per user per month[25]

While these costs are not trivial, they can be a savings over having to purchase, install, and maintain the software and all of the hardware (e.g., servers and disk) associated with an on-premise CRM solution that would typically be capitalized. My advice again to CIOs is to do your homework and conduct an analysis of competitive vendors and models (cloud and on-premise). While the trends are clearly moving to SaaS cloud solutions, more traditional offerings are available for purchase and support.

Forrester Research notes five trends that will change SaaS sourcing in the future:

1. SaaS applications will finally get an industry flavor. They'll expand their "industry editions" in the future and change their go-to-market strategy. Some vendors such as Oracle already sell multiple flavors to industries such as the high-technology, automotive, and life sciences.
2. Analytics modules will embed decision-making capabilities into SaaS. In the near future, SaaS solutions will include business intelligence (BI) and analytics *inside* or *packaged with* their offerings. This will be helpful to new organizations coming into SaaS that don't have mature BI or analytics departments. Those that do will need to rethink and potentially retool their BI or analytic strategies and move from on-premise, in-house solutions to the cloud as well or bring in the data from the cloud.
3. Cloud orchestration means new channels for SaaS purchasing for multiple cloud solutions. Applications will become more readily available for integration, support, and billing.
4. SaaS will become social. Salesforce is leading the way on this effort, integrating many elements of the social network into all of its products. Forrester and I believe that other SaaS vendors will quickly follow suit and converge social media into their applications.
5. Mobility will extend the real-time advantage of SaaS. Mobile access will drive more data and better analytics. Browser-based SaaS solutions will quickly evolve to include mobile applications so that their customers can access their products and solutions from anywhere.[26]

Major Players in the Cloud Market

There are a variety of IT advisory and market research firms that can expand on the major players helping to drive and shape the cloud marketplace today. Below is my list of companies that are leading and innovating. This list is by no means exhaustive, but it offers a glimpse into this broad and diverse market. I also offer an IT advisory glimpse into this marketplace later in this section. Here are the major players:

- **Salesforce.** This is one of the primary leaders in the cloud space, specifically focusing on SaaS. Not many vendors have adopted the *no software* claim from the beginning and innovated the way that Salesforce has after 14 years in the marketplace. Salesforce, like many other SaaS vendors, do offer plug-ins, which are installed on customer computing devices, where appropriate, to assist with other features, often messaging integration via an Outlook plug-in.
- **Google.** Google was an early adopter of the cloud, starting out with search and advertising before quickly expanding into e-mail, social, and collaboration SaaS offerings. Recently, Google has gotten into the mobile computing market as well, with PDAs and tablet offerings.
- **Microsoft.** Microsoft has steadily been moving products into the cloud that were traditionally installed on company computers and servers. It's most popular e-mail system, Exchange, is now available in the cloud and is hosted and managed by Microsoft rather than a third-party vendor. Office 365 is yet another example of this vendor's commitment to cloud computing.
- **Rackspace.** This is a leader in the PaaS and IaaS space, with solid offerings in both the public and the private cloud. Rackspace has spent the last couple of years building one of the most robust cloud infrastructures on the market. This definitely suggests a competitive look, compared to Amazon's EC2, and in some cases it is more expansive.
- **Amazon.** This is a leader in Web services and storage solutions. Amazon offers its customers flexible cloud computing options and was a pioneer in the elastic cloud model.
- **Apple.** Apple has always been one of the most innovative companies on the planet. Its evolution from cloud-based music services and digital music players to mobile computing and cloud applications is truly remarkable. It still seems to focus primarily on the consumer rather than the corporate enterprise, but that has clearly recently fueled the consumerization of IT and the "bring your own device" (BYOD) trend. Apple now stands as one of the most valuable companies in the world.
- **Oracle.** Oracle has been an innovator for years, starting with database technology, moving to business applications, and expanding into the cloud with several offerings (developed and purchased). Oracle remains one of the most aggressive companies around, with lots of revenue and money to spend on acquisitions. Don't count it out as a major player in the cloud market in the years to come.

- **IBM.** IBM has traditionally been an equipment manufacturer that led to software services through some key acquisitions of consulting service firms to a global infrastructure and application management services vendor. It was a little late in the cloud market (IaaS and PaaS) but will likely catch up quickly, and it will remain a force in the future.

Other notables are Apptix, CenturyLink, NaviSite, Terremark (Verizon), MindSHIFT Technologies, Cisco/WebEx, Box, RightNow, DropBox, Workday, NetSuite, Mozy, EMC, SAP, M5, and Citrix. There are thousands of vendors and products in the cloud space. Research before you buy, and pay attention to the terms and conditions, especially the out clauses, so that you can migrate to another solution if necessary.

Forrester Research notes the following leaders in the CRM suite as of Q3, 2012: Oracle Siebel CRM, Salesforce, Microsoft, RightNow, SAP Business All-in-One, SAP CRM, Oracle CRM On-Demand, and Pegasystems.[27]

The Security and Risks of Cloud Computing

Cloud computing has spawned brand-new issues and challenges for IT CIOs and CISOs to solve, such as integration and a renewed focus on data security. Just a few years ago, IT organizations typically had most of their data and applications in-house or on-premise, within their own data centers and control. We spent most of our security efforts protecting the *inside* trusted data network from the risks *outside* our firewalls.

Today we have a systems infrastructure (server, SAN, network, and security) inside and outside our organizations though a combination of public and private clouds. Our internal data centers form a security triangle with data at rest and data in transition within the corporate trusted network combined with private cloud (likely via dedicated circuits of secure VPNs) or public cloud offerings, most notably SaaS applications. There are several trends worth highlighting here:

- Security of information and data is now front and center for the CIO, with information residing in multiple locations and in transition via a variety of interfaces.
- Hardware services (SAN and servers) have become commodities and are quickly moving to the cloud. Cloud vendors are doing a better job at provisioning infrastructure and platform services than they were just a year or two ago and are now doing it well elastically or on demand, with performance also on demand.
- Content filtering tools are moving from blocking tools to information tools. Just a few years ago, many organizations blocked social media,

application sharing, file sharing, and collaboration sites because of security risks. Today application sharing, file sharing, and collaboration sites are flourishing, being purchased at a rate and a volume sometimes outside the IT budget and purchase authority and creating an information risk alert.

- DLP technologies are evolving to include mobile devices and social media. I strongly believe that DLP software, along with security provisions (and compliance with security certifications), will play a large role in the awareness and risks associated with an organization's data in the future.

Security Certifications

Security standards are helping to make cloud computing more secure. There are a number of certifications and standards used in the industry today and adopted by SaaS and cloud vendors. Security is the number one reason that some organizations avoid adopting cloud technologies. Vendors who leverage standards and comply with certifications can help customers overcome the security-concern hurdle. The following highlights a few certifications that cloud vendors are adopting today:

- **ISO 27001.** This standard replaced the old BS7799–2 standard as the specification for an information security management system (ISMS). The objective of this standard is to "provide a model for establishing, implementing, operating, monitoring, reviewing, maintaining, and improving an information security management system."[28] The standard defines the approach and contains sections related to management responsibility, internal audits, security management system improvement, control objectives, and controls.
- **ISO 20001.** This is a standard that's based on "a set of structured best practices and standard methodologies for core IT operational processes such as service, relationship, resolution, and release."[29]
- **Federal Information Security Management Act (FISMA).** This federal act promotes the development of key security standards and provides guidelines to support the implementation of the act and protect the nation's critical information infrastructure.[30] The U.S. government has been slower than other governments to migrate to the cloud; it was hesitant to do so until more concrete security best practices and standards were developed so that cloud vendors could certify their compliance before the government migrated certain services and data to the cloud.
- **Payment Card Industry Data Security Standard (PCI-DSS).** This standard was developed by the major credit and debit card networks

(American Express, Visa, MasterCard, and Discover) as a set of re-quirements of use payment processing components and commerce over the Internet. Compliance with this standard is based on levels, which are associated with the transaction volume of commerce per year and come with different sets of requirements and guidelines, de-pending on the level of volume of commerce conducted.

- **Statement on Standards for Attestation Engagements (SSAE) 16.** This is a statement of auditing standards (SAS) known as SAS 70. SSAE 16 was born of the older SAS and put into place around 2010. SSAE defines an organization's systems and control objectives and in-cludes an assertion by management that the controls were in place and applied during the most recent review period.[31]

These standards and certifications can be very complex and labor-intensive to comply with. A book or two could probably be written just on IT standards and certifications alone, so I refer you to the standards organi-zations that oversee these compliance standards and acts for more detailed information. The standards and certifications are a critical help to cloud ven-dors in making the case to CIOs and CISOs to move their data and applica-tions to the cloud and in assuring these executives that their solutions are relatively secure.

Security Risks and Mitigation

Cloud vendors have had their fair share of security issues and outages. Drop-box, Box, LinkedIn, Facebook, and Google have all had issues in recent years, but the major cloud-related problems have been more about outages than data breaches.[32] As more enterprise resources move to the cloud, security profes-sionals expect to see larger and more frequent security breaches in the future.

Recent Security Snafus

I'll highlight a number of issues, but note that there are many more and some that simply go unreported. The following is a sampling of recent data security issues experienced by cloud computing vendors:

- Mega-upload. The Federal Bureau of Investigation (FBI) raided the cloud file sharing and storage site, based in Hong Kong, on piracy charges. Outraged users of the site were encouraged by hackers to at-tack law enforcement and industry web sites supporting the raid with a denial-of-service attack.[33] Later, it was determined that some users were merely tricked into downloading Trojan software from infected sites.

- In January 2012, Zappos disclosed that hackers had broken into its network and stolen customer information, including personally identifiable information (PII).[34]
- In February 2012, the University of Florida had to notify a small group of individuals that their social security numbers had been improperly stored on a state web site for more than six years.[35]
- Also in February 2012, Foxconn, a large Asian company that makes Apple products, was hacked into by a group called Swagg Security, which was protesting poor working conditions in China.[36]
- Sony suffered more than a dozen data breaches of web sites shortly after it had laid off many of its security personnel.[37]
- In April 2011, Epsilon fell victim to a spear-phishing attack that compromised an "estimated 60 million customer e-mail addresses."[38]

Many more cloud vendors have had disruptions of their services caused by a variety of problems. Customers and businesses should get used to these types of security and outages, because the more vendors that host services in the cloud, the more often they may be targeted for security- and data-related breaches. That seems to be the nature of the hacking industry today.

Content Filtering and Data Loss Prevention

The best approach to dealing with security in today's hybrid environment is to have a defined strategy: determine your cloud approach and vendors, your integration strategy and tools, your monitoring detection, and your DLP. I recommend selecting prominent cloud vendors who are subscribing to today's more modern standards and guidelines and who are typically larger and more experienced in dedicating the appropriate resources to secure their customers' data.

I also recommend the use of content filtering and DLP software in order to know what the risks are and where your data are going. Content filtering tools can be very helpful in identifying just what IT or cloud services your users are using (sometimes without IT approval or funding). DLP software is complex and still evolving, but it can also help to identify the risks associated with data loss, theft, and leakage in today's social and cloud systems. DLP software can develop signatures that are constantly scanned throughout an organization's computing resources to determine whether a signature threat or a risk has been tripped and potentially blocked.

An example of how DLP could help is to develop a signature that traps the selection of key fields from your customer database in bulk. Detection is key, since without it you would not know that someone in the organization—with or without appropriate access—has done a full selection of your customer database and is about to write it into a data key, publish it on a private social media or file storage site, or send it to a personal e-mail account. DLP would most likely be able to sense the threshold violation, send an alert, and potentially block the transfer of the content outside the organization.

Implementation of DLP is not trivial, and it requires other considerations for it to work as intended. Some of the tough decisions that organizations will need to make is whether cloud vendors or products can be accessible by the staff on personal devices outside the corporate trusted network. This is a common request for ultimate flexibility, especially with the proliferation of personal devices in today's companies. However, if DLP can't monitor the device, it can't protect the information passed through the device.

As a result, to truly protect an organization's data in a social, cloud-based world of file storage, SaaS solutions, CRM solutions and collaboration solutions outside your data center requires tireless planning and policy considerations, many of which will annoy your user and staff base. I therefore believe that many organizations are less secure today than in previous years because they have succumbed to end-user pressure to lighten security provisions and policies—like BYOD and access to SaaS solutions via personal devices outside the management and control of IT.

Mark my words: Data security will be an issue for the next decade as the trend to the cloud continues and as standards and security software and tools attempt to catch up. I recommend the following to improve security in your organization as you move to the cloud:

- Assess cloud vendors carefully and research their histories for any security violations along with their compliance to newer security standards and guidelines. Request certification reports *before* you buy (e.g., SSAE 16, PCI, or FISMA). *CIO* magazine recommends that you ask cloud vendors the following 10 questions before you buy from them:
  1. Were your services deployed using a secure development cycle?
  2. Can you prove your security and provide certification and penetration test results?
  3. What data protection policies do you have in place?
  4. What are your data privacy policies?
  5. How do you enforce those various policies?
  6. Is security covered in your SLA? If not, why not?
  7. How do you back up and recover data and keep it secure?
  8. How do you encrypt data, both in motion and at rest?
  9. How do you segregate my data from others' (customers')?
  10. What kind of visibility will I have into your security logs?[39]

- Develop a security strategy and set of policies that takes into consideration cloud computing and SaaS solutions. This will likely require a full education effort to make your staff aware of the risks. Best-practice organizations are moving to include IT security training in their annual compliance training programs.
- Develop an incident response plan that has procedures and touch points with key executives in the organization in the event that a security or data theft or loss issue is reported.
- Consider obtaining cyber-liability insurance to hedge against an incident that can cause reputational or financial damage and loss.
- Reconfigure content filtering technology to report on data-related activities that occur across the Internet. Simply blocking social media sites will not resolve the risks associated with those platforms if your organization allows personal devices to be connected to your messaging systems, which is common today. Content filtering tools can become an important alert and a potential blocker of where your confidential data is being stored outside your organization.
- Consider DLP software and stronger IT policies for SaaS solutions that require access from company assets and computers that IT can verify are running the latest version of DLP scanning software.
- Train your IT staff on the risks and tools associated with cloud computing. They will be the gatekeepers to implementing your policies and technical solutions that protect your organization's sensitive and confidential information.

Integrating with the Cloud

The typical architecture today includes internal data centers, storage, applications, and cloud vendors (PaaS, IaaS, and most commonly SaaS) via private and public cloud computing environments. Exhibit 7.8 highlights the ease with which organizations can now have information in multiple places, requiring a different approach for integration.

Cloud Integration

The move to the cloud requires a new approach to integration. Some of the new tools that can assist with this transition come from the following vendors:

- IBM: Cast Iron
- Dell: Boomi
- Software AG: WebMethods
- Pervasive: Data Integrator

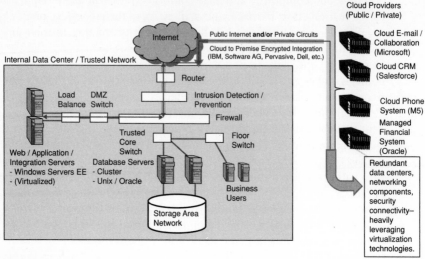

Exhibit 7.8   Cloud Computing

Exhibit 7.9 denotes the shift in integration strategy, tools, and approach and highlights the use of new integration enterprise bus middleware solutions that link cloud-to-cloud, cloud-to-on-premise, and on-premise-to-on-premise solutions securely with the same tools—and, if necessary, through encryption and in real time.

Cloud integration tools like IBM's Cast Iron allow developers to integrate solutions securely through a series of connectors. In many cases, buying an integration tool like Cast Iron or Dell's Boomi is worth the price of the

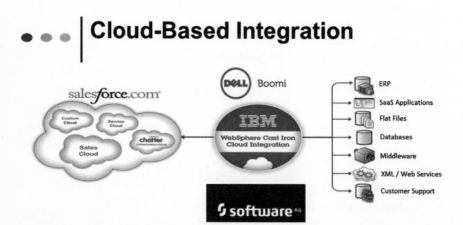

Exhibit 7.9   Cloud-Based Integration

adapters, not just the software that allows integration orchestration development between systems, whether cloud or on-premise. Cast Iron offers adapters for many of the leading ERP software vendors like Oracle, Microsoft, and Salesforce. The connectors are able to connect prebuilt Web services offered by the cloud vendor solutions through a new integration technique.

Integrations can be scheduled or performed in real time. Teams under my supervision and management have used tools like this to build real-time integrations that are encrypted between a Salesforce CRM SaaS cloud offering and a private cloud-hosted Oracle Financials solution. Solutions are typically priced as licensed software, include annual maintenance, and can run on virtual appliances or physical appliances. The decision to use a virtual server, or cloud versus a physical appliance, typically depends on the anticipated integration volume and load.

I asked my executive and CIO expert group for their thoughts about cloud computing and the associated risks. Their answers are eloquently stated in the following CIO survey.

CIO SURVEY

Do you use cloud computing services today in your organization? If so, public or private cloud?

- Yes. We have a few applications in the cloud at this time, but we do not have a strategy to make a wholesale move to the cloud. Generally, most applications are hosted on-premise. For every new project we undertake, we make decisions based on the business requirements, support and management being the key requirements. We find the solution that best meets our needs, whether it is cloud, SaaS, or a hosted model. Our analysis seems to indicate that ease of recoverability, availability, and better support are offset by the lack of flexibility, higher costs, and the actual quality of support. I believe the size of an organization is an important factor in deciding whether to use cloud services. If the organization is small with limited IT staff, then the move to the cloud model is compelling.

- Public and private. We are offering e-mail as a private cloud service to our international field offices.

—*Anne Topp, CIO, World Wildlife Fund*

(Continued)

CIO SURVEY (*Continued*)

- Yes, it is starting to take off.
- Both public and private cloud resources are used.
—*David Swartz, CIO, American University*

- Yes—absolutely critical to remain competitive.
- Both public and private.
—*Joel Schwalbe, CIO, CNL Financial Group*

The preponderance of CIOs I asked answered with a resounding *yes*.

What are the top drivers for implementing cloud services?

- Cost savings.
- Performance of specific functions better managed outside [our organization].
- Participation in business activities with external business partners that is better managed on neutral soil.
- Experimentation with limited risk fringe functions internally.
—*Martin Gomberg, former CIO; SVP and Global Director, Business Protection, A&E Networks*

- Speed to market for solutions that are the generic versions (cloud-based versions) can provide 75 percent or more of the functionality and can be deployed with much less cost, managed risk, and predictable change.
- A unique capability that IT does not have, could not build cost-effectively, or could not maintain in a cost-effective manner.
- Commodity services that are low-value, high-development, or operational-cost and low-risk. Solutions like help desk, fleet management, or even data processing can fall into this category.
—*Ed Anderson, International CIO, World Vision International*

- Efficiency—allowing the IT team members to focus on adding strategic value instead of maintaining platforms.

- Reducing development cycles and feature implementation time frames (substantially).
- Reducing disaster recovery or business continuity dependence on internal IT solutions.
- Note: Financial savings was not in our top three [criteria for selecting cloud].

—*Joel Schwalbe, CIO, CNL Financial Group*

How do you mitigate security concerns and issues associated with cloud computing services?

- As a CIO in a prestigious organization, I had to continually add staff members to an IT group dedicated to security. We were constantly barraged with attempted network intrusions. As a cloud consumer, you should believe that if you pick the right cloud computing organization with the right security and detection systems and processes in place, you will still be ahead of the game in terms of exposure and cost.

—*Carol F. Knouse, SVP and COO, EduTuit Corporation*

- We are beginning with functions or cloud services that are low-risk, commodity services. We began with these in order to get the value but also to learn the business issues (SLAs, contract terms, and so forth) as well as how to mitigate the security concerns. We are looking at cloud services and subjecting the vendors to our security processes and controls.

—*Ed Anderson, international CIO, World Vision International*

- CNL's General Counsel has established standards concerning the confidentiality of CNL's information—any cloud provider must meet those standards or is not considered eligible. CNL IT participates with the Office of the General Counsel in this process. Storing or sharing personally identifiable information (like social security numbers) is limited or not allowed in the cloud environment, depending on the requirements.

—*Joel Schwalbe, CIO, CNL Financial Group*

Clearly, the cloud market is an exciting one, with SaaS, IaaS, and PaaS vendors leading the way toward a fundamentally shifting IT market.

What Did I Do to Prepare?

Cloud computing is here to stay. IT professionals and CIOs need to adjust their thinking about cloud vendors and solutions, because your customers will be pushing you toward it. Market forces, what other organizations are doing, and the trends of IT changes have tremendous effects on what other organizations do. I suggest taking a cautious and measured approach to the cloud. The following are what I've done to prepare:

- I researched cloud vendors and strategies *before* forming a cloud strategy. IT leaders moving to the cloud need to understand the prerequisites and risks before going there. The most common and easiest move to the cloud is via SaaS. Most CIOs I've spoken to are already there, with several applications running in the old ASP model.
- I developed a cloud strategy a couple of years ago and implemented it after educating other C-level executives on the risks and advantages. Risk levels and tolerance will play a large role in how fast and how much information is pushed outside an organization's control. Research, ask a lot of colleagues, and, if necessary, get IT advisory advice from the best firms in the industry.
- I completely revamped my strategy for integration and opted for a cloud integration that allows cloud-to-cloud, cloud-to-on-premise, and on-premise-to-on-premise with the same tool.
- Pay attention to security. I've doubled down on newly minted security policies, incident response plans, and the overall approach to content filtering and DLP software. Security and integration will be a major focus for CIOs for the coming decade as a result of the shift into the cloud.

Recommendations

My recommendations for this chapter are as follows:

- Research some of the leading cloud vendors in the market. The most notable are Google, Microsoft, Salesforce, IBM, Rackspace, Amazon, Box, Workday, EMC, Cisco/WebEx, SAP, Mozy, M5, DropBox, NetSuite, and Citrix.
- Interrogate potential cloud vendors on security *before you buy*. Leverage IT advisory reports and advice on what to ask. I like to go with mainstream and larger organizations rather than smaller cloud vendors because of their investment and compliance with security.

Organizations need to weigh the appropriate risks before selecting a cloud vendor.

- Consult your IT advisory research firm for the best advice on selecting, negotiating contracts and SLAs, and managing secure integration as a result of the push to cloud computing.
- Determine your strategy for on-premise, public cloud, and private cloud in coordination with other C-level executives. Risk-averse CIOs will opt for on-premise and SaaS solutions (and secure integration to on-premise solutions). Risk-aware CIOs will opt for SaaS and private cloud offerings. Risk-open CIOs will push more of their applications, data, and infrastructure into the public and private clouds. Develop and refine your cloud strategy as part of the IT strategic plan. Share it with other C-level executives as part of the socialization of that plan.
- Conduct a financial analysis and ROI calculation before you leap to the cloud. Examples include options on purchasing software licenses for installation on-premise (via capital) versus a leased model in the cloud through SaaS (with operating expenses). Understand the differences and effects on budgeting and net income before you implement your cloud strategy.
- Lower-risk cloud offerings include SaaS. Higher-risk investments include the private cloud offerings PaaS and IaaS. Because of the potentially high investment for large infrastructure environments, I recommend that CIOs and their deputies do a detailed cost analysis and ROI calculation before investing in PaaS or IaaS. Find out which is better for your organization before leaping and make sure you include the total cost of ownership, which includes maintenance fees, staff dollars, and benefits.
- Revamp your integration strategy depending on your cloud strategy. Consider the following vendors as some of the best in the industry: IBM, Pervasive, Software AG, and Dell.
- Prepare your C-level colleagues and your staff for outages. They are inevitable, and moving to the cloud doesn't mean that you'll increase the uptime for your systems. Publish your SLAs for internal and external cloud solutions on your corporate intranet as a full example of a performance goal and transparency.
- Reshape the use of content filtering tools for information and consider implementing DLP software to truly know where your data are going outside your network.
- Coordinate with your general counsel on acceptable risks. Legal risks will trickle down to IT security policies, strategies, and technologies. Make no mistake—data risk in an organization is a legal department

issue for decisions and an IT department issue for implementation and monitoring. Don't get caught owning the risk decisions in IT.

- Determine your risk for personal devices (discussed later in this book), since it will impact your risk profile and your security strategy as it relates to cloud computing. The more you shift to free use of personal devices, the more you should increase DLP software and content filtering. Consider IP range solutions to ensure that devices that access your company's data are included in the security suite of software that your CIO and CISO decide to deploy. You'll know only about the data issues you can see. Personal devices are simply a risk to data security and theft. There—I said it, even as I've also gone kicking and screaming toward accepting BYOD.

Notes

1. Albert Einstein, Inspirational Quotes, www.inspirational-quotes.info/success-quotes.html (accessed October 1, 2012).
2. "Cloud Computing Glossary," Cloud Times, cloudtimes.org/glossary (accessed October 2, 2012).
3. Ibid.
4. "Platform as a Service (PaaS)," TechTarget, searchcloudcomputing.techtarget.com/definition/Platform-as-a-Service-PaaS (accessed October 6, 2012).
5. "Cloud Computing Glossary."
6. Ibid.
7. Ibid.
8. Ibid.
9. Doug Washburn, "Executive Spotlight: Top Priorities for IT Infrastructure & Operations Leaders, 2H 2011," Forrester Research, September 16, 2011.
10. Ibid.
11. Rackspace, www.rackspace.com/cloud/private (accessed September 10, 2012).
12. Andrew Reichman, "File Storage Costs Less in the Cloud Than In-House," Forrester Research, August 25, 2011.
13. James Staten and Lauren E. Nelson, "Master 10 Trends for Your Cloud Journey," Forrester Research, May 10, 2012.
14. Facebook, Key Facts, newsroom.fb.com/content/default.aspx?newsAreaId=22 (accessed October 15, 2012).
15. Twitter, blog.twitter.com/2011/03/numbers.html (accessed January 1, 2013).
16. Andrew Bartels, "Global Tech Market Outlook for 2012 And 2013," Forrester Research, January 6, 2012.
17. Ibid.
18. Amazon, EC2 Pricing, aws.amazon.com/ec2/pricing (accessed October 15, 2012).
19. Ibid.
20. Ibid.
21. Rackspace, Cloud Servers Pricing, www.rackspace.com/cloud/public/servers/pricing (accessed October 15, 2012).
22. Ibid.

23. Salesforce, salesforce.com/crm/editions-pricing.jsp?70130000000FJ27&internal=true (accessed October 15, 2012).
24. Ibid.
25. Ibid.
26. Liz Herbert, "Five Trends That Will Change SaaS Sourcing," November 30, 2011 (Cambridge, MA: Forrester Research).
27. "CRM Suite Customer Service Solutions, Q3, 2012," Forrester Research (accessed October 15, 2012).
28. 27000.org web site, "An Introduction to ISO 27001 (ISO27001), www.27000.org/iso-27001 .htm (accessed October 6, 2012).
29. Qpsinc.com web site, "ISO 20,001: IT Service Management Systems," www.qpsinc.com/ documents/ISO%2020001.htm (accessed October 6, 2012).
30. NIST web site, "Federal Information Security Management Act (FISMA) Implementation Project," csrc.nist.gov/groups/SMA/fisma/index.html (accessed October 6, 2012).
31. "SSAE 16 vs. SAS 70—What You Need to Know and Why," Statements on Standards for Attestation Engagements, www.ssae16.org/white-papers/ssae-16-vs-sas-70--what-you-need-to-know-and-why.html (accessed October 6, 2012).
32. Jeff Vance, "What You Really Need to Know about Cloud Security," *CIO*, June 18, 2012, www.cio.com/article/print/708649 (accessed July 20, 2012).
33. Ellen Messmer, "The Worst Security Snafus of 2012—So Far," *Network World*, July 13, 2012, www.networkworld.com/news/2012/071312-security-snafus-260874.html (accessed October 6, 2012).
34. Ibid.
35. Ibid.
36. Ibid.
37. Mathew J. Schwartz, "6 Worst Data Breaches of 2011," *Information Week*, December 28, 2011, www.informationweek.com/security/attacks/6-worst-data-breaches-of-2011/232301079 (accessed October 6, 2012).
38. Ibid.
39. Vance, "What You Really Need to Know about Cloud Security."

CHAPTER 8

The Consumerization of IT

Arguing with a fool proves there are two.

—Doris M. Smith[1]

Let me start this chapter with the following statement about the consumerization of IT that is so often repeated by my colleagues in the IT industry: "It's a challenge that adds risk and, in many cases, costs to an organization's IT governance and overall management of technology."

Consumer Devices Permeate the Corporate World

Consumer devices are impacting IT departments and organizations today with a rapid pace of adoption. Not long ago, IT organizations and CIOs were able to stand their ground in not allowing personal devices on the trusted corporate network. Today the proposition has turned 180 degrees, in favor of the consumer and *not* IT and legal executives.

According to Forrester Research, consumerization is the dominant force in smartphone and mobile device selection today; it has a simple definition:

- The device choice is made by the employee, not the organization or IT.
- The confirmation that employees are willing to assume some of the burden, if not all of it, for costs and support of the devices they choose to use in their personal lives and now at work.[2]

Forrester reported in a recent survey of 1,751 U.S. workers that bring your own device (BYOD) is real, with large percentages of employees paying for both the device acquisition (48 percent) and service (40 percent) but only 14 percent sharing ongoing usage costs with their employers through a reimbursement or stipend model (see Exhibit 8.1).[3]

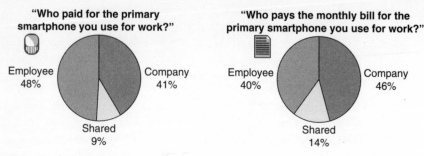

Exhibit 8.1   Bring Your Own Device Is a Reality Today
Source: Forrester Research

Consumer devices come in a variety of shapes and forms. The most common devices, from some of most innovative and exciting manufacturers, include the following:

- **Tablet computers.** Apple's iPad leads the way on this front. Google's Nexus 7 device is a competitive challenger, followed by tablets from Amazon (Kindle), Samsung (Galaxy) and Research in Motion (Black-Berry Playbook). Hewlett-Packard has reemerged into this market with the announcement of the ElitePad 900 Windows 8 tablet. Nokia Corporation is set to release a Windows 8 tablet in 2013 that will be available on the AT&T network. Tablets come in a variety of shapes, sizes, and operating systems, ranging from Windows to Google's Android to Apple's iOS. It is precisely the variation of vendor and operating system mix that can make these devices costly and difficult to support for IT departments today.
- **Laptops.** Traditional laptops are still the mobile computing device of choice for power users who travel frequently. I've yet to see a tablet fully replace a well-equipped laptop for hard-core work, but it may be coming in the future, likely via a laptop-tablet hybrid.
- **Laptop-tablet hybrid**. Hewlett-Packard's Envy X2 is an 11-inch tablet that comes with a keyboard dock with some high-end features like Beats Audio, pen support, and a high-resolution display. Microsoft also introduced the Surface hybrid running the Windows 8 operating system. I expect more hybrid devices to hit the market in the coming months and years.
- **Smartphones.** All one needs to do is search for "smartphone" on any search engine to see the myriad of vendors, products, features, and operating systems within this space. Today's smartphones, previously called PDAs, are highly functioning minicomputers that do voice, data,

applications, and video. They are the most common mobile device in the market today, with a staggering growth rate. I'll highlight some specific trends for smartphones later in this section, since they continue to be the predominant mobile computing choice today for both consumers and business professionals.

This market is extremely fierce and competitive and relies heavily on consumers to upgrade their equipment or model when a newer model becomes available and hits the shelves. I need not go beyond the Apple iPhone to highlight this behavior. My own children have upgraded their smartphone models as they have been improved.

There are essentially three schools of thought on how to deal with the onslaught of consumer devices today:

1. Block *anything* that's not purchased, configured, allocated, and supported by the IT department. Organizations that are risk-averse typically determine the mobile computing standard after testing, support, and purchase options are well examined and deploy updates to the standard from time to time—keeping with the traditional IT support model of "only support what's on the financial books and owned by the organization." In many cases, companies in highly regulated industries will dictate the policy on devices, since monitoring, logs, and information must be maintained in order to be compliant with specific industry regulations. The financial sector is one such place where the adoption of personal devices has been slow to come to fruition.

2. Allow *certain* personal devices to be integrated into the organization. This model evolves the IT standard approach and allows partial adoption of new devices that are approved by IT, but only after testing and confirmation that they can be properly supported with mobile device management (MDM) software and that they don't introduce excessive risks to the organization because of a lack of specific features, such as security. Organizations that employ this model typically require the staff to sign a series of acceptance forms stating the terms of what the organization can and cannot do, such as install software, monitor the device, and wipe it clean if it is lost or stolen. Support by the IT department under this option varies all the way from none to complete.

3. BYOD—allow *any and all* personal devices to be used to access organization systems and data, either in the cloud or through the organization's firewall to the trusted network. There are various policy options and processes for implementing BYOD, ranging from allowing all personal devices without any employee-signed acknowledgment to

requiring staffers to sign an agreement (with terms that are typically advantageous to the organization and not the individual) *before* they connect their devices to the corporate network or systems.

The effect of adding consumer devices to the corporate world typically means the following:

- Device selection affects the platforms (e.g., device, operating system, security, and ease of integration) that IT may integrate with the systems and information to be competitive and support the organization's information needs. One of the benefits of standardization (including with mobile devices) is that IT can ensure that the devices deployed will be properly supported by and integrated into the organization's systems. Letting consumers and staffers select their devices of choice doesn't always ensure that possibility.
- Mobile device selection usually affects the demands for computers in the organization. Once the gates are open to BYOD for mobile computing, the most common push for expansion is into the computers the employees use in their workday. Thus, bringing in a personal iPhone may result in a request for a nonstandard Macintosh computer next.
- The willingness of employees to absorb some or all of the costs affects the budgeting and expense reimbursement process within organizations—in many cases, making more work for the accounting department. With a central IT standard, the IT department typically pays for the device acquisition and usage, centrally budgets for those expenses, and either centrally pays for those services on a monthly basis or charges the departments with some frequency. A BYOD policy that puts all of the expenses on the employee is the easiest to implement from a cost perspective. Sharing expenses can have profound effects on how organizations budget and pay for services, often requiring each department to budget for its portion of mobile device usage and for accounting to process many more transactions per month than just one associated with a central IT standard method. As a result, there are hidden costs, many of them labor-associated, with a cost-sharing BYOD program that involves labor and time for budgeting and reimbursements. I've said, "Nothing is free, and if it is, it won't last forever" before. It applies here as well, especially for organizations that get involved in partial reimbursement for personal mobile device purchase and use.[4]

The following positions and recommendations discussed in a variety of articles highlight just how much consumerization of IT and BYOD is having an effect on managing technology and security in organizations today.

Consumerization Pros

- According to a recent Forrester Research report, "The days of IT-controlled smartphone deployments are over. Consumerization is the dominant force in smartphone selection."[5]
- According to a *CIO* magazine article, BYOD shifts the costs to the employee and away from the employer, in some cases as much as $80 per month per device. The article cited a recent survey of 600 U.S. IT and business leaders that found the following:
  - "A staggering 95 percent" of respondents permit employee-owned devices in the workplace.
  - Mobile devices are even happening behind closed and trusted network doors. Juniper Networks reported more than 4,000 users and professionals.
  - Virtualization giant VMWare went "all-in" with BYOD smartphones for its employees.
  - The most surprising finding in the report was that 41 percent of all respondents who use their personal device for work are doing so *without permission* from the company.[6]
- Worker satisfaction and flexibility is increased by BYOD because employees get to use the devices they want.[7]
- The devices are typically more cutting-edge and feature-rich in a consumerization or BYOD environment where employees can opt for the latest device as soon as it's released onto the market.[8]

Consumerization Cons

- Device compatibility with systems is not controllable by IT.[9]
- There are often hidden administrative costs (e.g., budgeting, expense tracking, or legal) associated with implementing a BYOD policy.[10]
- "There are issues of compliance and ownership when it comes to data" for mandates such as PCI-DSS, the Health Insurance Portability and Accountability Act (HIPAA), or the Gramm-Leach-Billey Act (GLBA).[11]
- Security and device management is more challenging and costly for IT departments as a result of a nonstandard or expanded standard with BYOD.

The result, according to Gartner Research, is that the consumerization trend is "driving IT shops crazy." The report states that "the number of devices coming in the next few years will outstrip IT's ability to keep the enterprise secure." In addition, MDM software is helpful to monitor and manage which devices have access to certain applications, but it is "not a secure enough approach." DLP software may be one of the more promising tools in the future to help organizations protect their data in the rapid trend to allow personal devices in the corporate world.[12]

Growth Trends for Mobile Computing

Market share *is* important in today's computing environment, especially the mobile platform and device market. In the first edition of *Straight to the Top*, I noted that software developers write to the market share. This is still true, and it has been highlighted with some dizzying reversal of fortunes (and market share) for some of the mobile device vendors selling their wares. Just a few years ago, Research in Motion (RIM), which makes the BlackBerry smartphone, was at the top of the corporate world and could do no wrong. That was also when most CIOs wouldn't even consider allowing a personal device to penetrate their corporate networks to access systems and data within their control.

Today, RIM is hanging on for its life. It is not totally down and out, but market share has absolutely turned against the company, and it is the market share that developers still consistently write toward. Blackberry 10, released in January 2013, is RIM's last chance to regain market share and stay alive. Just the other day, I was having a conversation with a cloud security vendor who also had a DLP product, and I asked about support for the BlackBerry. The answer was "Not yet, and we're not sure if we'll press ahead with the product on the BlackBerry in the future." I asked what order the vendor developed its products for and the answer was swift: iOS (Apple), Android (Google), and Microsoft as the distant third. Interestingly enough, that's very close to the current market share leaders in order.

Global mobile phone and smartphone usage is also rising rapidly, accelerating the effects of the consumerization of IT impact on organizations around the world with 6.1 billion phone subscriptions, and approximately 1 billion of these are advanced smartphones.[13]

The explosive growth affects several key vendors, some of which are on the rise while others are reducing their market share percentages. Exhibit 8.2 shows mobile growth by vendor from 2007 to 2012. Google's Android devices and Apple's iPhone experienced the most significant growth.[14]

In looking at the projected worldwide sales of Internet access devices, including tablets and smartphones, between 2010 and 2014, tablets are expected to grow tenfold, from 20 million to 208 million (see Exhibit 8.3). Smartphones continue a more linear growth pattern, from 240 million devices in 2010 to a projected 800 million, a threefold increase. Laptops and computers are projected to maintain a slow and steady increase,

Exhibit 8.2   Smartphone Sales Trends

Year	Android (Google)	BlackBerry (RIM)	iPhone (Apple)	Palm/ WebOS	Symbian (Nokia)	Windows Mobile (Microsoft)
2007		11.77	3.3	1.76	77.68	14.7
2008		23.15	11.42	2.51	72.93	16.5
2009	6.8	34.35	24.89	1.19	80.88	15.03
2010	67.22	47.45	46.6		111.58	12.38
2011	219.52	51.54	89.26		93.41	8.77

from 352 million in 2010 to 545 million in 2014.[15] What's interesting is that regardless of the significant trends in mobile computing, with smartphones leading the way as the device of choice, laptops and computers hold their own in a clear second place, on the way to 1.5 billion mobile devices by 2014.

When comparing the adoption of Google Android versus Apple's iOS shipments from the launch of each product, Android demonstrates the clear lead with four times adoption when compared to the iPhone.[16]

According to Gartner, Android operating system devices command a 72.4 percent market share as of Q3, 2012, followed by Apple's iOS (13.9 percent), RIM (5.3 percent), Bada (3 percent), Symbian (2.6 percent), and Microsoft (2.4 percent).[17] IT advisory firms and research I've followed indicate that the predominance of smartphone market share, up to 90 percent, will be shared by Android devices, Apple, and Microsoft. Whether RIM can challenge Microsoft for third place is still a question, but I've invested a little bit of money, holding out hope as a BlackBerry fan.

Even toy manufactures are getting in on the mobile computing craze. Toys "R" Us unveiled a $150 tablet for children called the Tabeo that features a seven-inch screen and a Wi-Fi connection and comes preloaded with 50 kid-friendly applications.[18]

Exhibit 8.3   Tablet vs. Smartphone vs. PC Growth Trends

Devices	2010	2011	2012	2013	2014
PC	352 million	409M	450M	495M	545M
Tablet	20M	55M	80M	120M	208M
Smartphone	240M	350M	450M	650M	800M
Total	612M	814M	980M	1.2 billion	1.553 billion

Behavior changes in the market are fueling the shift into mobile computing. Some recent examples are the following:

- **McDonald's.** The fast-food chain's customers in Paris, France, can now pay for products using a smartphone or a tablet computer, a strategy that could spread across the chain's 33,000 or more locations, if the results are positive.[19]
- **Nordstrom.** Clothing retailers like Nordstrom have plans to go completely mobile in its stores, outfitting employees with Apple iPod Touches and other devices capable of taking credit cards. Nordstrom is looking to benefit by reclaiming valuable floor space that is currently devoted to registers.[20]
- **Grocery stores and food companies.** According to the *Wall Street Journal*, U.S. food companies are reaching children by embedding their products and messages in "simple and enticing games for touch-screen phones and tablets."[21] Companies are deploying games such as Cookie Dough Bites Factory, Super Pretzel Factory, and Icee Maker that kids download and play, in an attempt to influence buying patterns through their parents when they go shopping. The cost associated with making a game that's downloaded hundreds of thousands of times, compared to traditional advertising runs in print and television, is allowing the companies to experiment with new methods to reach customers and prospects, potentially at a lower acquisition cost.
- **Commerce.** Square's card reader, which charges a small percentage per swipe, is exploding onto the mobile device market, allowing small and medium-size businesses to take credit on the go. My taxi driver now has one, and so do several small businesses in my area. However, the system is compatible only with Android and Apple's iOS, not BlackBerry. Remember market share?

These are just a few examples. There are hundreds more like them. Organizations are using technology—specifically, mobile, cloud, and social media—to increase revenue, lower costs, learn more about their customers, and reach them through the devices and channels on which they want to interact.

Forrester Research offers the following predictions on mobile computing:

- One billion consumers will have smartphones by 2016. U.S. consumers alone will have 257 million of them, along with 126 million tablet computers.
- Apple, Google, and Microsoft will account for more than 90 percent of the platforms used in smartphones and tablets worldwide.

- Carriers will compete for wireless spectrums that support 5.8 billion public Wi-Fi hot spots.
- Of the projected 257 million smartphone users in the United States, 200 million will use their personal devices at work.
- Mobile spending will reach $1.3 trillion as the mobile application market reaches $55 billion in 2016. At an average price of $2.43 per application, the growth will explode to $56 billion in 2015 as more owners tap into applications.
- Business spending on mobile projects will grow by 100 percent by 2015.[22]

Get ready for the continuation of a wild ride. Now let's talk about how organizations are going to manage all of these devices in the future. It's called mobile device management, or MDM.

Increasing Costs and Security

Mobile device use and security are increasing with the combination of BYOD and IT department deployment. Newer smartphones that have the ability to access rich graphical and video information are using far more bandwidth than before and increasing the usage costs as a result—potentially for both personal and corporate assets. Telecommunications carriers are deploying more sophisticated networks to handle current and anticipated growth in data, including large volumes of video as more and more people use their smartphones to watch their movies or highlights from the evening news.

Mobile devices are the primary means by which individuals access their personal and corporate e-mail, use social networking sites, videoconference with their friends, use GPS services for travel, get their news, and even still make phone calls. According to the leading Internet security firm Websense, "Your social media identity may prove more valuable to cybercriminals than your credit."[23] Since more mobile devices today are both personal and corporate, the security risks include corporate data as well as personal data. The Web statistics and highlights are troubling for security, especially for the U.S. user, for the following reasons:

- The United States is the top country for phishing attacks.
- The United States is the top country hosting malware.
- The United States is the top country for malware redirects to other sites.
- Mobile devices are "subject to threats accessing web and e-mail content, and humans remain the weakest security link in the chain." It is reported that 51 percent of users turn off device passwords and security controls on their mobile devices.

- Since the Android platform is an open operating system where anyone can contribute an update, the environment is rife with security concerns. Of the 200,000 Android applications analyzed by Websense Labs, noticeable percentages were found to have malicious intent.
- Data loss and theft remain the primary security concerns to reduce risk with lost or stolen devices.[24]

Several different strategies are emerging and available on the market to help organizations deal with mobile security. Device management software, security awareness training for staff, device passwords, content filters that extend to mobile devices, and DLP technologies are some viable opportunities. No one solution or approach will guarantee the security of confidential and personal data. I'd like to focus on one of the more important tools within IT departments to make devices more secure: MDM.

Mobile Device Management

According to *CIO* magazine, MDM software allows organizations to mandate encryption, set and enforce policies for applications, provision and deprovision applications and data, and even wipe devices clean in the event of a lost or stolen device or a terminated employee. Many in the industry believe that MDM will evolve from controlling the device to controlling the data in a short period of time. In terms of BYOD, MDM can be invaluable to IT departments because they can set up configuration and security to deal only with information and applications that are relevant to the organization. It would be difficult to tell BYOD users that they can't use iCloud or the AppStore on their own devices. Rather, MDM lets IT control the data and applications and make sure that corporate data aren't leaking into personal applications and services like DropBox.[25]

For BlackBerrys, the BlackBerry Enterprise Server is the gold standard MDM application, with well over 500 individual policies for configuration and enforcement of mobile devices. Despite RIM's one-time leadership in market share and MDM, organizations adopting BYOD and other devices or operating systems need to look to solutions that can secure their information. Forrester highlights the critical functionality needed in today's MDM solutions:

- Scheduled and event-based actions.
- Real-time inventory information on installed applications, security settings, and configuration.
- Remote control.
- Self-service portals.

- Security management, including personal identification number (PIN) enforcement, passwords, data wiping, data encryption, and ActiveSync device restriction (to prevent users from accessing the corporate network without approval from IT).
- Application purchase restrictions.
- Advanced monitoring, alerts, and reporting.[26]

An entire book could be written on mobile device security, so I'll just conclude this section with vendor and product recommendations from Forrester Research.

Incumbents
- Good Technology
- Microsoft ActiveSync
- RIM
- Sybase

Innovators
- AirWatch
- BoxTone
- MobileIron
- Zenprise

Some of the vendors sell on-premise and hosted solutions. Not all vendors offer mobile platform support for all of the major products, including Android, iOS, BlackBerry, Symbian, Windows Mobile/CE/Phone 7, and WebOS. Please conduct your research carefully and, if possible, pilot an MDM product before you buy it.

I asked my distinguished IT executive advisory team members to provide their insights on the consumerization of IT. Please see their answers in the CIO Survey below on how they are dealing with the growing mobile trend.

CIO SURVEY

Does the consumerization of personal devices affect you in any way regarding IT governance and management?

- We do not allow personal devices on our infrastructure, so not at this time. It will be a discussion in our governance process as we begin to study the cost, effect, and implications of BYOD on the

(Continued)

CIO SURVEY (*Continued*)

organization. The governance board will have to make a decision on the cost versus risk of this approach.

—*Ed Anderson, International CIO, World Vision International*

- Yes, it does. As people bring more devices to work and demand accessing work information from them, it is becoming a nightmare to manage those devices and the data going through them. We mainly let them access corporate mail systems at the moment through personal devices and don't have any governance methodology yet.

—*A. Murat Mendi, CIO, Ulkar Holding*

- Definitely. Just a few years ago, most corporate data was housed on corporate resources or devices. That is no longer true. With the need to access data from anywhere, at any time, on any device, security management has changed dramatically. However, I am not sure that the business executive's view on security has changed appropriately. While IT recognizes that corporate data are now housed on many personal devices, I believe many business leaders have a false sense of security about digital information.

- It is the consumerization not only of devices but also of services. DropBox and other commercial file-sharing technologies have made it hard for IT to safeguard data. There is little management and visibility into what is being shared and with whom. Business e-mail is often synchronized, forwarded, or downloaded to personal e-mail accounts. Remote access technologies such as Citrix allow staff to download files to personal devices. USB keys can transfer terabytes of data from business devices to personal devices.

- There may be tools to allow an organization to lock down the computing environment, but the cost to the organization in real dollars, in support costs, and in the resulting lack of flexibility will influence how much risk the organization can accept. Each organization will have to determine its own risk profile and then devise an appropriate level of governance.

- The new age of consumerization will make businesses rethink how they do business and to what degree they want to safeguard their data. This is not an IT decision. IT's role will be to help identify vulnerabilities, educate the business with regard to the risks, and then implement technical solutions to mitigate those risks. In this new world, technical solutions will need to be implemented in conjunction with strategies from the human resources, legal, and finance departments.

—*Anne Topp, CIO, World Wildlife Fund*

- Yes—the biggest issue is security. How do we ensure that personal devices being used to access corporate IT resources will not be infected with viruses and other problems as a result of personal downloads from a myriad of web sites? The way in which we control that is we have arrived at a set of devices that are approved for use: only those devices supplied and secured by the company can be used to access our resources.

—*Carol F. Knouse, SVP and COO, EduTuit Corporation*

- Yes, it can, unless the appropriate tools, policies, and safeguards are in place from inception. CNL was an early adopter of MDM software and has been running it for over 18 months. We're moving toward a BYOD environment, and we do support BYOD when the associates sign a release waiver and allow certain software to be installed on their devices to protect CNL's content.

—*Joel Schwalbe, CIO, CNL Financial Group*

- Yes. I have not moved to a BYOD model, although we are now more flexible in permitted technologies than before. I am considering a stipend-based store model where employees can procure approved technologies, which they then own, with stipends based on level and minimal retention before the devices can be recycled. Something like that could be a cost savings, minimize frivolous turnover requests, and not conflict with a BYOD strategy. In theory, it could even be used to balance individuals' spending by giving

(Continued)

CIO SURVEY (*Continued*)

them the option to allocate their stipends as they see fit on furniture upgrades and desktop or mobile technologies, managing within a personal budget. It would be interesting to see if I could get this type of model approved and off the ground.

—*Martin Gomberg, former CIO; SVP and Global Director, Business Protection, A&E Networks*

From the input of my advisory group of IT executives and from my discussions with other CIOs, it's clear that there is no simple and consistent answer when it comes to allowing and supporting personal devices in the corporate environment. Clearly, the effect of consumer and personal devices on the CIO and IT in general exists today and is expected to have an even greater effect on purchasing, support, and security in the future.

This is a battle that CIOs need to be prepared to fight from a device management perspective but lose from a BYOD perspective. The gates have already been opened with regard to mobile computing use, and the trends are clear: social media, cloud computing, and the rapid innovation occurring today in the mobile device market (e.g., smartphones and tablets) is driving the clear trend toward mobile computing. It's here to stay. CIOs need to integrate mobile into their strategies and strike a balance between allowing personal devices and security. There is no holy grail on this subject.

What Did I Do to Prepare?

I've done the following to prepare for the consumerization of IT:

- Researched adoption trends and metrics for mobile devices today and incorporated the information where appropriate into our IT standards.
- Accepted BYOD but developed some clear parameters for support and financial reimbursement.
- Developed a mobile strategy as part of the IT strategic plan.
- Developed a tablet pilot and focused time and effort on deploying mobile applications developed specifically for mobile devices.

- Investigated MDM tools and forged ahead on implementing a solution.
- Clarified support and SLAs for corporate and personal devices.
- Reshaped the organization's security policy and developed a new incident response plan (IRP) that includes provisions for the loss or theft of sensitive data.
- Retained options for higher levels of security, including DLP.
- Researched MDM solutions before deploying a pilot and installing.

Recommendations

My recommendations for this chapter are as follows:

- Working with your general counsel, develop a risk profile, and adopt the appropriate technologies and policies to meet that profile. Organizations that are willing to consider personal devices and BYOD should do so after a full analysis of the costs and risks. The policy communication should be done through the general counsel and the CIO. Risk is a legal decision, not an IT one. The CIO is responsible for implementing controls to meet the organization's risk profile, not to define it. That's the legal department's job.
- Develop a mobile strategy as part of your IT strategic plan.
- Carefully craft or modify your tablet strategy as part of your mobile strategy and be sure to clarify any intersections with a BYOD plan. I believe laptop-hybrid tablets will emerge as viable options for businesses and larger organizations that are concerned with manageability, security, performance, and, most important, compatibility with legacy and supported applications. Notables include Apple iPad, Dell XPS, and Microsoft Surface. As others enter the market, evaluate them carefully. A safer strategy may end up being a multidevice standard to satisfy user demand while maintaining device management flexibility.
- Develop a security strategy and wrap it around mobile devices (corporate ones and personal ones that contain corporate data). Update your security policies and procedures as necessary and train your staff on the new security risks, including mobile. Security should move from the device to the data.
- Research and deploy MDM tools as part of the toolbox for managing mobile devices, including personal assets not owned by the organization. AirWatch, BoxTone, MobileIron, and Zenprise are top products. Good Technology, Microsoft ActiveSync, RIM, and Sybase are notables. Some of the vendors sell on-premise and hosted solutions. Evaluate what's best for you and your organization. Not all

vendors offer mobile platform support for all of the major products, including Android, iOS, BlackBerry, Symbian, Windows Mobile/CE/Phone 7 and WebOS, so check your research carefully and, if possible, pilot an MDM product before you buy it.

- Clarify your support for personal devices and stick to it. Don't set an SLA expectation that you can't meet, especially if you're limited on the number of IT resources to provide tier 1 and tier 2 support.
- Look for simplified internal policies on budgeting and expense allocation for BYOD. There are easy ways and hard ways to do this. The hard ones will reveal themselves through a clear increase in time, labor, and the number of transactions processed by accounting.
- Consider DLP software to alert the organization's key departments (legal, financial, human resources, and IT) about the loss or theft of corporate information—intentionally or unintentionally. Mobile computing is a fast-growing security problem for CIOs and CISOs today.
- Forrester Research and other IT advisory firms have some great research on the usefulness of tablets in the enterprise and whether they can replace or augment the computing gear provided and supported by the IT department. The growth numbers of tablets and smartphones combined with the expected resilience of the laptop computer in the future indicates that there's no holy grail device that will do everything. Forrester Research has some super reports that expose the real and valuable use of tablets like the iPad, their costs, and whether they will be the main device carried by staffers or just one of several, carried along with a smartphone and a laptop. I very often see employees with three devices each: a personal smartphone, a corporate laptop, and a mix of personal and corporate tablets. There is a real cost to having that many devices in the workplace. There's also a higher security risk to loss of confidential data, especially when all of these devices, corporate and personal, are connected to an organization's technical systems.

I'll leave it at that. The research will prove to be some great reading for those who love to jump onto new technologies but not necessarily to have to pay to secure and support them.

Notes

1. Doris M. Smith, Inspiration Quotes, www.inspirational-quotes.info/people.html (accessed October 6, 2012).
2. Ted Schadler, "Consumerization Drives Smartphone Proliferation," Forrester Research, December 2, 2011.

3. Ibid.

4. Ibid.

5. Ibid.

6. Tom Kaneshige, "CIO Challenge with BYOD: Don't Fall Down the Rabbit Hole," *CIO*, May 17, 2012, www.cio.com/article/print/706579 (accessed July 20, 2012).

7. Tony Bradley, "Pros and Cons of BYOD (Bring Your Own Device), *CIO*, December 21, 2011, www.cio.com/article/print/696971 (accessed July 20, 2012).

8. Ibid.

9. Ibid.

10. Ibid.

11. Ibid.

12. Matt Hamblen, "Consumerization Trend Driving IT Shops Crazy, Gartner Analyst Says," *CIO*, May 2, 2012, www.cio.com/article/print/705448 (accessed July 20, 2012).

13. Mary Meeker, "Internet Trends—D10 Conference," Kleiner, Perkins, Caufield, Byers (KPCB), May 30, 2012, www.kpcb.com/insights/2012-internet-trends (accessed September 1, 2012).

14. Jyoti Patodia, "It's Raining Tablets and Smartphones," Motley Fool, September 11, 2012, beta.fool.com/jyotiadvisor/2012/09/11/its-raining-tablets-smartphones/11794/ (accessed September 12, 2012).

15. Ibid.

16. Meeker, "Internet Trends—D10 Conference."

17. Harsh Chauhan, "Which Also-Ran Will Run the Fastest in the Smartphone Race?" The Motley Fool, beta.fool.com/techjunk13/2013/01/02/which-also-ran-will-run-fastest-smartphone-race/20414/?logvisit=y&published=2013-01-02&source=eptcnnlnk0000001 (accessed January 3, 2013).

18. Julianne Pepitone, "Toys R Us Unveils $150 Tablet for Kids," *CNN Money*, September 10, 2012, money.cnn.com/2012/09/10/technology/toys-r-us-tablet-kids/index.html (accessed September 9, 2012).

19. Doug Gross, "Fries from Your Phone: McDonald's Testing Mobile Payment App," CNN, (August 20, 2012), www.cnn.com/2012/08/20/tech/mobile/mcdonalds-mobile-payments/index.html (accessed August 20, 2012).

20. Rolfe Winkler, "Mobile Devices Hit Retail Pay Dirt," *Wall Street Journal*, September 18, 2012, C12.

21. Anton Troianovski, "Hook Kids on Mobile Games," *Wall Street Journal*, September 18, 2012, A1.

22. Ted Schadler and John C. McCarthy, "Mobile Is the New Face of Engagement," Forrester Research, February 13, 2012.

23. "Websense Threat Report 2012," *Websense Inc.*, 13.

24. Ibid, p. 28.

25. Thor Osavsrud, "For BYOD Best Practices, Secure Data, Not Devices," *CIO*, July 17, 2012, www.cio.com/article/print/711258 (accessed July 20, 2012).

26. Christian Kane and Benjamin Gray, "Market Overview: On-Premises Mobile Device Management Solutions," Forrester Research, January 3, 2012.

CHAPTER 9

Social Media Changes Everything

The real voyage of discovery consists not in seeking new landscapes but in having new eyes.

—MARCEL PROUST[1]

Social media can best be described as a conversation that takes place online through a set of tools that can include text, audio, video, and pictures. Some say it's the future of communication. Leading companies, like Facebook and LinkedIn, have created platforms for online communities where individuals can share information about themselves in private or to the public.

Social Media Categories

There is a variety of social media types, broken down by the following categories:

- **Social networks.** Facebook, Google+, LinkedIn, Twitter, and so on allow users to search, link to other individuals or groups, and share information (e.g., interests, contacts, or posts) in a private or public manner, typically called a *profile setting*. Facebook's "like" button allows users to indicate their preferences for content, albeit only positive, while Twitter allows bursts of 140 characters to "followers."
- **Social sharing.** YouTube, Snapfish, Flickr, and so on let users share specific types of content, such as videos and pictures, publicly and privately.
- **Social news.** Sites like Digg and Newsvine publish recent news topics and let users vote and comment on articles.

- **Social bookmarking.** Sites like Delicious and Reddit allow users to find and bookmark information that's of interest, access it from anywhere online, and share it with others.

Social media use has exploded in recent years and has moved from being a social conversation to being about business. Companies are using social media to connect with prospects and customers and to run social media campaigns designed to drive awareness of a brand, cause, or mission or to simply sell more products. The following (repeated from Chapter 2) are some of the growth trends and statistics associated with social media and networking today:

- About 68 percent of Americans using social networks in 2011 indicated that none of the networks influenced their buying.
- In 2012, 47 percent indicated that Facebook had the greatest effect on purchase behavior.
- Twitter users are 33 percent more likely to be Democrats.
- The fastest growing segment in social media is 45- to 54-year-olds.
- About 54 percent of Facebook users access the site via a mobile computing device, and 33 percent of the users access the site as their *primary* mechanism.[2]

Some additional and more recently researched factoids and interesting statistics are as follows:

- Social media have overtaken pornography as the number one activity on the Internet.[3]
- One in five couples meets online.[4]
- One in five divorces is blamed on Facebook.[5]
- About 69 percent of parents are "friends" with their children on social media sites.[6]
- The top five Twitter personalities with the largest followers are Lady Gaga, Justin Bieber, Katy Perry, Rihanna, and Britney Spears, with 29.8 million, 28.4 million, 27.1 million, 26 million, and 20.7 million followers, respectively. President Barack Obama comes in at number six, with 20.3 million.[7]
- If Wikipedia were made into a book, it would be 2.25 million pages long.[8]
- About 90 percent of consumers trust peer recommendations, while only 14 percent trust advertisements.[9]
- About 93 percent of marketers use social media for business.[10]
- About 25 percent of the search results for the world's 20 largest brands are linked to user-generated content.[11]

Here are some job-related social media statistics from the Millennial Branding and Beyond Multi-Generational Job Search Study:

- Online job searches are conducted by an overwhelming majority of every generation: baby boomers (96 percent), Gen X (95 percent), and Gen Y (92 percent).
- Google and Google+ is the preferred social network for both Gen X and Gen Y, while LinkedIn is the top choice for baby boomers.
- The length of a job search is the greatest for baby boomers, followed by Gen X and Gen Y, with 25 percent of baby boomers looking for more than a year.
- Between 5 and 20 hours per week are spent by all generations on job searches, with 19 percent of baby boomers spending between 20 and 30 hours per week.[12]

There are various usage statistics for the major players in social media. According to the GlobalWebIndex, while Facebook has a clear lead in the United States, Google+ is popular with BRIC (Brazil, Russia, India, China) nations with 38 percent of users in India, 29 percent in Turkey, 28 percent in Brazil, 25 percent in China, and 25 percent in Russia—with users accessing the site at least once a month in Q2 of 2012.[21]

I read a really funny comment about social media: "What happens in Vegas stays in Vegas, unless it's posted on YouTube, Flickr, or Facebook." Let that serve to remind many of us that the Internet is a vehicle to spread information like wildfire—good and bad. I'll highlight several of the worst disasters with the assistance of social media later in this chapter.

Social Media Titans ✳

Who are the titans of social media? Some of the top social media titans are profitable, while others are not. Take Twitter, for example. It has figured out how to capitalize on its 500 million user base to turn advertisements into increasing profit, which is projected to grow from 44.6 million in 2010 to $807 million by 2014, (see Exhibit 9.1) all while offline advertising continues to shrink.[13]

Google dominates advertising in the mobile space, but several other social media companies are seeing gains with advertising on mobile devices as well. According to eMarketer.com, Google leads in advertising revenue on mobile devices with an estimated $1.5 billion in 2012 and a projected $3.6 billion in 2014. Compare this to estimate projections for Pandora ($200 million in 2012, $500 million in 2014), Twitter (100 million in 2012, $425 million in 2014), and Facebook ($73 million in 2012, $629 million in 2014) (see Exhibit 9.2).[14]

Twitter's Ad Revenue Tipped to Double This Year

Estimated global advertising revenue of Twitter (in million U.S. dollars)

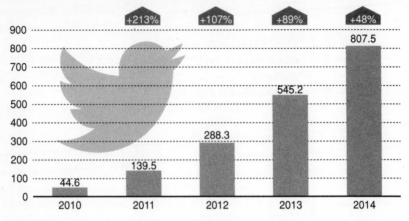

Exhibit 9.1   Twitter's Estimated Global Advertising Revenue, 2010–2014
Source: eMarketer

Facebook's Mobile Ads Are Expected to Take Off

Estimated U.S. mobile advertising revenues in 2012 and 2014 (in million U.S. dollars)

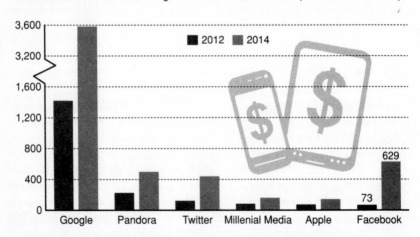

Exhibit 9.2   Estimated Mobile Advertising Revenues in the United States
Source: eMarketer

Based on my research, and taking into consideration the number of users, revenue, global reach, and functionality, my top 10 social media list consists of the following:

1. Facebook
2. YouTube
3. Wikipedia
4. Blogspot
5. Twitter

6. WordPress
7. LinkedIn
8. Google+
9. Instagram
10. Flickr

Social Media Are the World's Reporters

Social media platforms and sites have played such an important role in documenting history as it takes place. The speed at which information—text via Twitter, video via YouTube, and pictures via several social media platform sites—is staggering. I'll highlight three issues that helped to change the world, thousands of reporters or users at a time.

The Syrian Uprising

According to the Annenberg School for Communication at the University of Pennsylvania, "Social media and user-generated content (UGC)—photos and videos taken by members of the public—played an important role in coverage of the revolutions in Egypt, Tunisia, and Libya, but this was chiefly supplementary to traditional news gathering for covering those revolutions. However, in Syria, with tight control on foreign media denying access for foreign journalists, news organizations had to rely *almost exclusively* on UGC via social media and their own UGC intake platforms."[15]

It's possible to say that the public's coverage of the Arab Spring uprisings contributed to some of the government overthrows and revolutions in these countries. Social media played a large part and continue to play an important role in Syria, since the only foreign journalists in that country are likely to have crossed the border illegally. The Syrian people's coverage of the Syrian uprising demonstrates the will of the people to tell their stories. Many of the stories were told on Facebook, Twitter, and especially YouTube, which includes many videos of some horrific acts. Governments like Syria, North Korea, and China, which attempt to filter events through the Internet—inbound and outbound—will in the end most likely lose out to the sheer will of the people as they will find a way to get their stories out. Couriers, data keys, satellite transmissions, and recorded video on cell phones, can all find their way onto the social media stage and, if important enough, can spread like wildfire and drive a revolution of change.

But the role of social media is a double-edged sword, because it has been used by both sides in this conflict. The Syrian government and its supporters are extremely effective in using social media tools to track and discredit the protesters.[16] The Syrian government has spent billions of dollars for Western technologies to monitor Internet and e-mail activity, and it has also attempted to shut down the Internet, "cutting electricity and phone services."[17] In response, the Syrian people turned to proxy sites and mobile technologies not blocked by the government to get their message out to the world.

As I write this chapter, the Syrian rebels are continuing their attacks on the Syrian government, which in turn continues to slaughter the rebels and many innocent civilians. The world sits by and hopes that in the end, social media will play a similar role in toppling the Syrian dictator as in toppling the Tunisian and Egyptian dictators.

Hurricane Isaac: New Orleans

Social media played a positive role during Hurricane Isaac, which hit New Orleans in 2012. In advance, "the city set up a website and Twitter account to get information out as it becomes available.[18] The governor's office used Twitter to communicate and inform the public, sending out the following tweet:

> Gov@BobbyJindal: Authorized activation of up to 3,000 LA Nat'l Guardsmen if necessary for #Isaac; 700 fulltime Guardsmen are working today.[19]

Unfortunately, because of the rush to send out a message, it's not always worded as well as it could be. A *PR Daily* article suggested that the previous message could have been worded as follows:

> Gov@BobbyJindal: Authorized activation of up to 3,000 LA Nat'l Guardsmen if necessary for #Isaac *to make sure we keep people safe and protect their property*; 700 fulltime Guardsmen are working today.[20]

Throughout the hurricane, social media played a large role in communicating between the public and the government and, as a result, probably helped to save lives.

The Colorado Theater Shooting

One of the more disturbing activities in the last year or so was the shooting inside an Aurora, Colorado, movie theater showing the new Batman movie, *The Dark Knight Rises*, in which 12 people were killed and another 38 wounded.[21]

Before social media, the public would have to wait for the press or the police to report an incident like this. With social media, the incident unfolded in real time.

According to CNN, "The social media posts about the Colorado shooting are a haunting reminder of the visceral power of first-person accounts of a tragedy."[22] Several reports occurred as the shooting started. Here are some of the posts:

- "Now I'm thinking it was bullets coming through the wall from 9 causing smoke and fire cracker sounds. #aurorashooting #batman #shooting."
- "I am getting ready to cry. So scared. I need a hug. I almost got shot 9 times. I had a chance to be like 50."
- "I seen a person bleeding out their mouth and gasping for their last breath. This ain't right. #Century16Shooting."[23]

In reality, the social media play a significant part in people's lives, and since data seem to live on forever on the Internet, this technology is helping to document history *as it happens*.

There's also a downside to social media. An Iranian woman (Neda Agha Soltan) was killed in her country's 2009 uprising, and her picture was spread all over the Internet—only it wasn't *her* picture, it was the picture of a woman with a very similar name (Neda Soltani), who went through intense government persecution as a result and then had to flee the country, leaving everything behind: her family, her friends, and her job. In just 12 days, Neda Soltani's life was completely destroyed by a simple mistake, which spread like wildfire *despite her attempts to correct it*.

Businesses Using Social Media

Three to four years ago, when IT executives spoke about social media, they were most likely referring to how many social media web sites had been blocked by their content filtering solutions in an attempt to keep company information inside and raise the productivity of their workers. Today, companies that don't use social media platforms, marketing campaigns, and sites to service their customers will be out of business in five years—or at least be at a significant disadvantage in relation to their competitors. The driving facts are simple for IT and companies to engage in social media today: it's where the vast majority of your customers will be and what they will be using to communicate with you.

In addition to making money in the social media space by selling advertisements to users (browser-based and on mobile devices) or making games for people to play in their spare time, companies are now leveraging social media to communicate with their customers, find new markets and customers, and support and service their customers.

According to Forrester Research, the CMO is the most common executive leading social initiatives in companies today, but the CIO is becoming even more important as the implementer of those technologies and solutions. "Dynamic, flatter organizations built around social connections that focus on solving business and customer challenges are replacing old hierarchical organizations."[24]

Employees use social networking, Forrester Research notes, to stay up-to-date with news (84 percent), to get ideas for work (78 percent), to research information for work (77 percent), and to stay in touch with friends (75 percent). See Exhibit 9.3.[25]

Forrester Research suggests in this report that CIOs need to evaluate the current state of social business maturity and develop a plan to help the organization attain a higher maturity level. Best Buy, for instance, started a collaboration platform that enabled employees to solve customer challenges by sharing information and ideas. In coordination with the CMO, IT should do the following:

- Develop an IT social business team that serves as an advisory council on how the organization can use social media tools like Yammer or Twitter to solve a business challenge.

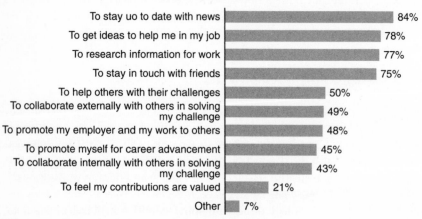

"What are the main reasons you use social media?"
(Check all that apply)

To stay uo to date with news	84%
To get ideas to help me in my job	78%
To research information for work	77%
To stay in touch with friends	75%
To help others with their challenges	50%
To collaborate externally with others in solving my challenge	49%
To promote my employer and my work to others	48%
To promote myself for career advancement	45%
To collaborate internally with others in solving my challenge	43%
To feel my contributions are valued	21%
Other	7%

Base: 337 social media users

Source: January 2010 Global Social Media Online Survey

Exhibit 9.3   Employees Use Social Technologies at Work to Increase Productivity
Source: Forrester Research, Inc.

- Hold social workshops for IT.
- Start an IT leadership blog.
- Consider video social media channels for training. Black & Decker uses video to create a learning library for sales.
- Challenge vendors with outcome-based contracts.[26]

By getting ahead of social networking, IT will be better equipped to team up with other business units that are developing and strategizing on the company's social media activities.

A number of innovative companies are using social media technology today. I highlight a few here, but note that hundreds more are making strides every day:

- **Top Shop.** The British fashion company developed a Facebook application that allows users to watch fashion shows and purchase the goods they're seeing in real time.
- **Game Stop and Activision.** Activision is using Salesforce's CRM and Service Cloud offerings to better support customers in the medium that customers want to be in: the social network. Customers can submit support requests via Facebook and Twitter to Game Stop, where they may have bought the game, if a user is having an issue. Game Stop is tightly integrated into Activision, the game maker, and can work seamlessly with Game Stop to get engaged if the store needs to pass the support request to the company. Activision can even tweet solutions to customers and interact with their customers via their mobile phone video chat.
- **Grey Poupon.** This company uses specialized social media software to conduct Facebook campaigns.
- **Salesforce's Marketing Cloud product.** This is one of a new wave of online marketing tools that companies can use to quickly develop, deploy, and manage social media campaigns—all with no software installed on the client's computer.
- **Red Robin.** When Red Robin introduced its new Tavern Double burger line, it turned to social media. "The 460-restaurant chain used an internal social network resembling Facebook to teach its managers everything from the recipes to the best, fastest way to make them."[27] The result has reduced the time it takes to collect information and feedback (previously done with spiral-bound notebooks in the mail) from months to days. Many other companies are using similar internal social technologies. The company I currently work at leverages a social media collaboration platform by Salesforce called Chatter.
- **eHarmony and Match.** These two dating services are pushing the envelope on creating a social community of "love candidates" with their

sites. Match developed an application that works with Facebook to browse photos of singles on Facebook and receive "winks" and messages *without leaving* the social media site.

- **Mercedes A Class.** The German car company created a cool video posted on YouTube as part of a social media campaign and asked the public to decide how the car chase ends by sending one of two tweets (#HIDE or #EVADE) to the company. The advertisement ran during the popular show *The X Factor*.[28]
- **Kellogg.** The company developed an adventurous campaign that involved a shop in London that allowed people to pay in tweets instead of money. The company was looking for word-of-mouth publicity, so it asked customers to send tweets plugging the brand if they wanted to receive a free pack of Kellogg's Special K crisps.[29]

There are thousands of cool examples of companies using social media today. The bottom line for companies is that if you're not social, mobile, and in the cloud, you may not be in business in the years to come, because your competitors will most likely be in the social media space. I encourage readers to troll through the myriad of reports that highlight some of the great things companies are doing today. And here's a tip: When you find a great article or report, share it with someone on your favorite social site.

The Risks of Social Media

There are several risks associated with using social media—in life and for business. I offer the following examples and a few highlights of some recent corporate brand blunders that raced like wildfire through social media channels:

- **Security of company information.** It's not uncommon that an organization's data go out the door. More of those leaks and losses are going through social networks. Examples include employees posting confidential content or negative information about their boss on a social networking site. If you don't think this is common, check out Glassdoor (www.glassdoor.com). Put your company name in the search box and check out the reviews and comments.
- **Inappropriate posts and tweets that spread like wildfire.** The streets are littered with many, many bad tweets and posts. During the first debate between President Barack Obama and challenger Mitt Romney in the 2012 presidential campaign, KitchenAid tweeted about the president's debate performance, saying, "Obamas

gma even knew it was going2 b bad! She died 3 days b4 he became president."[30] After posting this to the company's 24,000 followers, it quickly deleted the tweet and indicated that an employee had accidentally posted it from KitchenAid's account instead of his or her personal account.

- **Data privacy and theft.** Social media sites have been hacked, exposing personal and business information to hackers and the public. Mitigating this is tough, since many of the breaches occur within the social sites themselves and are exposed through weaknesses or vulnerabilities. DLP is a promising tool, along with content filtering solutions, to identify what and where your corporate data are going in the social blogosphere. As social media technologies have accelerated, this has become a full-time job for several IT resources.

- **Keeping up with the content and requests on your company's social media channels.** It's not enough that your company is in social media; realistically, this means that your company brand— along with rapid access to company employees—is represented via several social channels. Maintaining content, keeping up with conversations, and saying the right things are hard. CNN Money predicts that tweeting robots will be a tool used in the near future to assist with the social media information workload for companies. In 2011, United Airlines had the distinction of "ranking worst in social media sentiment among nine major airlines, with 55,000 negative tweets."[31] Social media has quickly gone from being a cool and effective resource for communicating with your customers to becoming a public relations nightmare that requires a lot of resources to manage the sheer volume of the social conversations taking place in a company's social media channels, costing way more in labor than anticipated.

- **Fake personas online.** You don't necessarily know who the person is online. In addition, others can easily set up similar social media channels on the same platforms and communicate an entirely different message in your name to the public. Legal teams often force fake sites to shut down before they damage the reputation and brand of a company. The fake persona also applies to individuals as followers or those who "like" your social media content. Unfortunately, people who hide behind fake personas and intentionally do damage are a reality on the Internet. Sometimes companies just have to be reactive to situations in which damaging claims or statements are made in the social space. It's a risk that will not go away. According to CNN, 83 million Facebook accounts are fakes and duplicates.[32]

I'll close out this chapter with a sampling of some of the worst brand blunders that were affected by or enabled via social media:

- **FedEx.** A video recorded by a home security system recorded a driver greatly mishandling an electronic package. That video went viral and became the butt of many jokes ending with "FedEx."[33]
- **Kenneth Cole.** The well-known shoe manufacturer attempted to take advantage of trending hashtags, but it backfired when the following message went out during the Egyptian uprising:

"Millions are in uproar in #Cairo. Rumor is they heard our new spring collection is now available online at http://bit.ly/KCairo-KC."

- **Chrysler.** A contract employee with New Media enraged Chrysler and its customers with the following tweet on the company's Twitter feed:

"I find it ironic that Detroit is known as the #motorcity and yet no one here knows how to f#*!ing drive."

- **StubHub.** The company claims that it may have been hacked after an offensive tweet was released stating the following:

"Thank f&#k it's Friday! Can't wait to get out of this stubsucking hell hole."

- **Domino's Pizza.** In 2009, before Domino's even had a social media presence, it "found itself in a difficult public relations situation after two employees in its Conover, North Carolina, franchise uploaded a video to YouTube of themselves doing disgusting things to a sandwich before it went out to delivery." The video went viral, and the pizza chain was put on an instant defensive position that resulted in several actions to deal with the issue, including an official video statement from the president of Domino's, Patrick Doyle.[34]

Facebook Fatigue?

Another problem is the fatigue associated with Facebook, the leading social media company. According to GlobalWebIndex, one of the world's global insight studies on consumer behavior, "The world's largest social has reached a saturation point among active Internet users in more markets, with significant user-growth restricted to emerging markets such as India, Indonesia, and Brazil." The study states that "declines in social networking activity such as messaging friends fell 12 percent, searching for new contacts fell 17 percent, and joining a group [fell] 19 percent among all Facebook users in the U.S."[35]

Fatigue will lead, at some point in the future, to another cool tool that comes along and knocks Facebook off the top of the mountain. It's not a matter of if, but when, as IT trends ebb and flow in the marketplace. Don't believe me? Remember MySpace?

We live in a crazy world that's social, fortunately and unfortunately. The tools, technologies, and trends are causing companies to think of creative new strategies for embracing the social media channels and platforms, all while protecting their brand and company assets, including data.

What's Next in Social Media

One thing that's consistently true in technology is that nothing stays the same. MySpace is almost a thing of the past and Facebook, while experiencing growth in certain geographical regions, is starting to wobble with certain user and feature segments showing fatigue.

According to social media management system HootSuite's CEO, Ryan Holmes, get ready for the following seven social media networks to watch in the year ahead:

1. **Pheed**. A pay-as-you-go social network mainly for celebrities, musicians, and other entertainment professionals. It has the option of charging users to follow premier content on their feed. Miley Cyrus and Paris Hilton are already up and running on the system.
2. **Thumb**. A personal crowd-sourcing site that allows large groups of users to give a thumbs-up or thumbs-down (and leave comments) such questions as does a particular shirt go with a specific pair of jeans.
3. **Medium**. An invitation-only social media site from the creators of Twitter, where content creators share deeper and more though-provoking stories with their audience. Creators are limited (by invitation), but the readers can be endless.
4. **Chirpify**. Buy merchandise with the word *buy* and simplify the checkout process so that the entire transaction is easier and conducted through a user's Twitter account. This site can also be used for fundraising, giveaways, and peer-to-peer payments. The site is currently free to use, but it takes a 5 percent cut anytime a person is paid.
5. **Flayvr**. A site that's intended to bring order to photo- and video-sharing collections via eye-catching "albums" that can be easily shared as an HTML5 web page.
6. **Chirp**. Members can share photos and messages from their smartphones via a two-second robotic squeak to other phones in the area

within audio range. Chirps "can be shared in a boardroom, or a crowded bar, broadcasted over loud speakers and even embedded in YouTube videos."

7. **Conversations**. A tool from Hootsuite that brings social networks into the office by allowing teams to collaborate in real time by posting on message boards. This may be a breakout tool for customer service and marketing teams who currently use instant messaging tools for similar but more limited functions.[36]

I asked my IT executive advisory team for its insights on social media. The insightful answers are included in the CIO Survey that follows.

CIO SURVEY

What is your social networking strategy? What specifically do you use Twitter and Facebook for as part of your social media strategy?

- Social media in a university is critical to reaching our students and alumni. We employ Facebook, Twitter, and LinkedIn, among others. We push content from our content management system to the Web and share it across the social media. We use it to help prospecting for new students and to firm relationships with alumni.

  —*David Swartz, CIO, American University*

- [We use social media for] intercompany social networking to connect and collaborate. [We do not] use Twitter or Facebook.

  —*Ray Barnard, SVP and CIO, Fluor*

- We use Twitter and Facebook for marketing, and the organization has been doing this for some time now. The biggest challenge has been determining the effectiveness of these tools. We use these tools to reach out to new donors, to inform existing donors, and to put branding messages and content into the marketplace. I think we are heavy on tool use and light on a comprehensive strategy.

  —*Ed Anderson, International CIO, World Vision International*

- Unfortunately, CNL operates in a highly regulated environment where social media is not allowed at this time (SEC and FINRA regulated). We ultimately see this changing as archiving and e-discovery applications for social media become more prevalent and generally accepted and approved by the SEC and FINRA.

—*Joel Schwalbe, CIO, CNL Financial Group*

- We do not yet rely on social media officially internally. I say "officially" because it would be naive to believe our folks aren't using it to communicate with colleagues already. We mitigate risks in this area through policy and education. Long-term, my peers and I have discussed embracing social media as the next step in our logical evolution of corporate communication and collaboration.

- Externally, we rely on both Twitter and Facebook to communicate with and incentivize our customers. This dialogue is bidirectional, and we attempt to glean insights and trend sentiments from our customers on our store conditions, their in-store shopping experiences, and our product offerings.

—*Joshua R. Jewett, SVP and CIO, Family Dollar Inc.*

What is the cost effect and revenue per year as a result of implementing your social media strategy? Is it worth the investment, and can you easily quantify an ROI?

- We track very closely our Web analytics to see how much traffic we are generating from social media and also mobile, which are the fastest-growing segments for our marketing efforts.

—*David Swartz, CIO, American University*

- [Revenue is to be decided at this time]. The cost is $2 to $5 million, and the ROI is under construction.

—*Ray Barnard, SVP and CIO, Fluor*

- We do not know at this time. We are trying to quantify the effect of social networking on revenue, but we see this as a cost of doing business (something we have to do whether or not there is tangible benefit). The marketplace expects it.

—*Ed Anderson, International CIO, World Vision International*

(Continued)

CIO SURVEY (*Continued*)

- Our investments at this point are modest, and the insight, while valuable, is difficult to quantify.
—*Joshua R. Jewett, SVP and CIO, Family Dollar Inc.*

Do you use Internet content filters to restrict staff usage of social media networking sites during business hours and ward off productivity and information security loss?

- No. A university is a very open environment. We do not filter or limit our staff, faculty, or students.
—*David Swartz, CIO, American University*

- Yes. [We block Facebook and Twitter.]
—*Ray Barnard, SVP and CIO, Fluor*

- We do not block social networking sites, but gambling, pornography, and so forth are restricted.
—*Ed Anderson, International CIO, World Vision International*

- Yes, [we block] but have recently decided to remove these controls for most sites. We'll still meter streaming video and block most peer-to-peer [traffic], but we will open Facebook, Twitter, and so forth. We're mitigating risks through policy and education.
—*Joshua R. Jewett, SVP and CIO, Family Dollar Inc.*

Some of the CIOs I spoke to admitted that their organizations were behind in regard to the social media networking trends and in strategies to leverage the rich content within them. This is not surprising to me, especially in sectors that are either heavily regulated or nonprofit. It does, however, inform me that there is still work to be done in IT and that while it's difficult to quantify the investment in social media technologies and campaign or marketing tools, it's likely to be an inevitable decision in the near future.

What Did I Do to Prepare?

Social media is such a large focus area that's moving so fast that it's hard to simply put a list of things I've done and make recommendations to readers. The following outlines what I've done in the social space lately:

- I've conducted a lot of research on the tools and platforms on the market. Also, knowing how other organizations are using social media helps me and others think of creative ways to use social technologies in our lives and organizations.
- I'm working with our internal communications team members on taking the social strategy to market.
- I've set up accounts on a number of social media platforms to leverage some of the power in this great medium. I must admit that not all of my accounts and profiles overtly spell out that it's me; I use an alias so that I don't get bombarded with sales attempts and shared information that will make me less productive in my life and my job. Sorry to the folks at LinkedIn—I just got too many sales calls with my name and title.
- I've used IT advisory reports and information from organizations like Forrester to advise my internal peers on strategies.
- I've attended social media marketing strategies and software demonstrations to learn how the new solutions are helping organizations to harness the power of the social network.
- I've worked with internal legal teams to craft the social media usage and technology policies. Pay attention to this advice and make sure your employees are aware of the policies through education.
- I'm looking at social media platforms for sharing IT training material.
- I utilize social media collaboration tools daily in my role as the CIO, from Salesforce's Chatter.

Recommendations

My recommendations for this chapter are as follows:

- Do a lot of research on the tools and platforms on the market. Ask vendors to come into your organization to demonstrate their social products as a means of sharing information with others in the organization regarding what's on the market and what other organizations are doing.
- Set up a social media team in IT and put the most social networking employees in the group. Share ideas on how your organization (IT and

the entire company) can leverage social media to improve a process, communicate better with a customer, or drive revenue and donations.

- Work with your marketing and/or communications team members on the social strategy in your company. Recognize that IT doesn't own it, but look to play an implementation and advisory role in the process.
- If you're not in the social space, get there and set up accounts and profiles on a variety of sites. Use an alias if you think that you'll get a negative experience by listing your full name and professional title and organization.
- Use IT advisory reports and information from organizations like Forrester to advise your internal peers on strategies.
- Attend social media marketing strategies, events, and software demonstrations to learn how the new solutions are helping organizations to harness the power of the social network.
- Get up to speed on your company's social media policy. If there's an opportunity, help to revise it and make it better and more current. The days when organizations block social media sites with their Internet content filters are quickly ending. It's not very smart to do that if the organization is leveraging the social network to drive revenue and connect or support customers.
- Consider social media platforms for sharing IT training material and look for opportunities to expand beyond IT.
- If you need assistance, find a really good social media marketing and technology consulting company. There's no need to reinvent the wheel here, and it's no different from hiring a good finance, accounting, or IT person with skills to do the job well.
- Understand the security elements that go with social media. If you have an opportunity to work on the IT team that's charged with security, get engaged. There are new tools to help organizations deal with the risks associated with social media. DLP is one such tool, and combined with information gleaned from content filters, it can provide even more information to assist with mitigation strategies.
- Research some of the newer social marketing tools. Salesforce's Marketing Cloud is a new entry that shows some great promise. Other notables include Shoutlet, Direct Message Lab, Objective Marketer, MediaFunnel, Hootsuite, and Sprinklr. Some heavy-hitting companies are using these products to do their social media campaigns.
- Put policies and procedures in place within your company for anyone who posts information on a social media site. Best practices include at least a second set of eyes as an approver. Doing so may mitigate the risks associated with some of the crazy posts and mishaps that have caused significant brand damage for companies around the world.

Notes

1. Marcel Proust, Inspirational Quotes, www.inspirational-quotes.info/imagination.html (accessed October 11, 2012).
2. Tom Webster, "Why Twitter Is Bigger Than You Think," Edison Research, April 24, 2012, www.edisonresearch.com/home/archives/2012/04/why-twitter-is-bigger-than-you-think.php (accessed August 3, 2012).
3. Belinda Goldsmith, "Porn Passed Over as Web Users Become Social," Reuters, September 16, 2008, www.reuters.com/article/2008/09/16/us-internet-book-life-idUSSP31943720080916 (accessed October 6, 2012).
4. "Stay Up to Date: Introducing the Official Match.com Blog," Match, blog.match.com/2010/05/17/stay-up-to-date-introducing-the-official-match-com-blog (accessed October 8, 2012).
5. Tony Cooper, "One in Five U.S. Divorces Fueled by Facebook, Social Media," *San Diego News*, March 1, 2011, local.sandiego.com/news/one-in-five-u.s.-divorces-fueled-by-facebook-social-media (accessed October 6, 2012).
6. Liberty Mutual, "Mamapedia Voices," Mamapedia, www.mamapedia.com/voices/placeholder-liberty-mutual (accessed October 13, 2012).
7. Twoplist—Global, Twopcharts, twopcharts.com/twoplist.php?source=gl (accessed October 13, 2012).
8. Erik Qualman, "39 Social Media Statistics to Start 2012," Socialnomics, January 4, 2012, www.socialnomics.net/2012/01/04/39-social-media-statistics-to-start-2012 (accessed October 13, 2012).
9. "Global Advertising: Consumers Trust Real Friends and Virtual Strangers the Most," NeilsenWire, July 7, 2009, blog.nielsen.com/nielsenwire/consumer/global-advertising-consumers-trust-real-friends-and-virtual-strangers-the-most (accessed October 13, 2012).
10. Michael Stelzner, "2011 Social Media Marketing Industry Report," Social Media Examiner, April 7, 2011), www.socialmediaexaminer.com/social-media-marketing-industry-report-2011 (accessed October 13, 2012).
11. Chris Aarons, Andru Edwards, and Xavier Lanier, "Turning Blogs and User-Generated Content into Search Engine Results," *SES Magazine*, June 8, 2009, 24–25.
12. Dan Schawbel, "The Multi-Generational Job Search Study," Millennial Branding, September 24, 2012, millennialbranding.com/2012/09/multi-generational-job-search-study (accessed October 13, 2012).
13. Felix Richter, "Twitter's Ad Revenue Tipped to Double This Year," Statista, September 13, 2012, www.statista.com/markets/21/topic/194/social-media/chart/608/twitter-s-global-advertising-revenue-from-2010-to-2014 (accessed November 11, 2012).
14. Felix Richter, "Facebook's Mobile Ads Are Expected to Take Off," Statista, June 9, 2012, www.statista.com/topics/751/facebook/chart/591/mobile-advertising-revenues-in-the-united-states (accessed November 11, 2012).
15. Juliette Harkin, Kevin Anderson, Libby Morgan, and Briar Smith, "Deciphering User-Generated Content in Transitional Societies: A Syria Coverage Case Study," University of Pennsylvania Annenberg School for Communication, March 2012.
16. Namo Abdulla, "Social Media and Syria's Revolution," Rudaw, December 20, 2011, www.rudaw.net/english/news/syria/4244.html (accessed August 31, 2012).
17. "Syria's Cyber Wars," Mediapolicy, June 1, 2012, www.mediapolicy.org/2012/06/syrias-cyber-wars (accessed August 31, 2012).
18. Matt Wilson, "How New Orleans Is Using Social Media to Prepare for Hurricane Isaac," *PR Daily*, August 28, 2012, www.prdaily.com/Main/Articles/How_New_Orleans_is_using_social_media_to_prepare_f_12519.aspx (accessed August 31, 2012).
19. Ibid.
20. Ibid.

21. John D. Sutter, "Theater Shooting Unfolds in Real Time on Social Media," CNN, July 20, 2012, articles.cnn.com/2012-07-20/tech/tech_social-media_colorado-shooting-social-media_1_shootings-last-night-twitter-user-social-media (accessed July 20, 2012).
22. Ibid.
23. Ibid.
24. Nigel Fenwick, "Social Business Strategy: An IT Execution Plan," Forrester Research, April 20, 2011.
25. Ibid.
26. Ibid.
27. Tim Mullaney, "Red Robin and Other Companies Are Using Facebook-Like Technology to Rethink the Old Way of Doing Things," USA Today, May 17, 2012, 1A.
28. "The Top 10 Social Media Campaigns from the UK," Simply Zesty, October 13, 2012, www.simplyzesty.com/social-media/top-10-uk-social-media-campaigns (accessed October 13, 2012).
29. Ibid.
30. "When Social Media Gets Ugly: The 20 Biggest Brand Disasters," Simply Zesty, October 11, 2012, www.simplyzesty.com/social-media/when-social-media-gets-ugly-the-20-biggest-brand-disasters (accessed October 13, 2012).
31. Ryan Holmes, "Here Come the Tweeting Robots," CNN Money, July 23, 2012, tech.fortune.cnn.com/2012/07/23/tweetbots (accessed October 13, 2012).
32. Heather Kelly, "83 million Facebook Accounts Are Fakes and Dupes," CNN, August 2, 2012, www.cnn.com/2012/08/02/tech/social-media/facebook-fake-accounts/index.html (accessed August 3, 2012).
33. When Social Media Gets Ugly—The 20 Biggest Brand Disasters," Simplyzesty.com, October 11, 2012, www.simplyzesty.com/social-media/when-social-media-gets-ugly-the-20-biggest-brand-disasters (accessed October 13, 2012).
34. Ibid.
35. "Facebook Fatigue Is Spreading but Social Media Is on the Rise, Says Internet Study," Next Web (GlobalWebIndex), February 6, 2012, thenextweb.com/socialmedia/2012/02/06/facebook-fatigue-is-spreading-but-social-media-is-on-the-rise-says-internet-study/?fromcat=all (accessed October 15, 2012).
36. Ryan Holmes, "7 Social networks to watch in 2013," CNN Money, January 10, 2013, http://money.cnn.com/gallery/magazines/fortune/2013/01/10/2013-social-networks.fortune/2.html (accessed January 11, 2013).

CHAPTER 10

What's after the CIO Role?

Exert your talents and distinguish yourself, and don't think of retiring from the world until the world will be sorry that you retire.

—SAMUEL JOHNSON[1]

Career Next Steps

As I prepared for this chapter, it struck me that CIOs spend so much time preparing for their executive IT role and doing it well that they don't think much about the next career step. When I look at the role itself, the number of years' experience it takes to ascend to the role, and the average number of years a CIO practices IT, it's no wonder many don't think beyond the role of the CIO—they retire. For those who are thinking about options, there are several.

Chief Executive Officer

According to *CIO* magazine, "It's a success indicator for CIOs who are taking on formal or informal responsibilities in non-IT aspects of the business or moving up to the CEO role." Traditionally, the CEO sets the criteria for performance throughout the organization and for most of the C-level positions. The article indicates that while good CIOs stand up well against their bosses and can even outperform them on occasion, a common gap is in the area of "strategic business leadership." It is this gap that CIOs aspiring to the role of the CEO need to pay attention to and focus on.[2]

According to Egon Zehnder International, a global executive recruiting company that has significant experience assessing executive talent, there are competency differences between CEOs and CIOs. Using a database of

25,000 executives with performance data based on 360-degree assessments, Egon Zehnder found the following key points:

- The top CIOs (those in the top 15 percent) scored highest in results orientation, strategic orientation, change leadership, and customer focus.
- The top CIOs performed better than average CIOs in all competencies except for people and organizational development, where they were equivalent.
- People and organizational development scores are relatively low for all types of executives assessed, especially CFOs.
- The top CIOs scored slightly higher than good CEOs on most competencies.
- The top CEOs, well-rounded strategic thinkers, performed much better than the top CIOs only in market knowledge and external customer focus.[3]

According to *CIO* magazine, CIOs who aspire to the CEO role should spend time honing their business strategy and innovation skills in addition to being solid change leaders, collaborators, influencers, and business experts. CEOs can often come from sales functions as a result of having close relationships with key customers and a focus on customers in general. The CIO, in contrast, spends most of his or her day on internal stakeholders, with little or no chance in some cases to spend time with prospective customers or key customers.[4] This is one of the main conundrums for CIOs today. They are focused internally, but if they aspire to be CEOs, they must learn to focus externally.

A CIO is likely to have more of a chance of becoming the CEO of a technical company than of an organization that does not produce or support a technical product or service. It's quite possible that a CIO with great industry knowledge, technical knowledge, and strategic vision could become the CEO of a cloud computing or an IT services firm, for instance. For a CIO to become the CEO of a nontechnical company is less likely.

Chief Operating Officer

One role that's well within the promotion space of the CIO is the COO. The COO role is often equated with the role of the CIO, primarily because both tend to an organization's business operations, mostly internal. The COO role often has human resources, finance and accounting, and facilities under its control in addition to IT.

Many of the skills required for CIOs today are inherent in the other operational functions. Great CIOs lead, motivate, and care immensely for the human capital component of their budgets and domains. CIOs who do not managing money well usually report to the CFO, so those who don't have to report to the CFO are assumed to be pretty good at managing money and handling large budgets and contract negotiations with vendors. IT and facilities continue to merge, with more and more facility functions becoming smart technology–based. CIOs and their data center managers need to be adept with power management, cooling electrical functions, and so on, which outside the data center traditionally fall to the facilities team.

As a result of the skills and oversight often provided by the COO and what good CIOs do as part of their normal career path, CIOs are very good candidates to become COOs—potentially in their current organizations through promotion. CIOs are typically good problem solvers. That skill transitions quite well to the role of a COO. In conclusion, I believe that CIOs who are looking for a continued career move outside IT will choose the COO position and succeed in it.

Other Options

Other options for CIOs beyond retirement are typically individual decisions and not part of a traditional career path that includes a higher C-level position. Only the individuals themselves know what they want to do once they've had enough of the IT sector. The following are some options that I've considered:

- **Think about being a teacher.** High schools can always use a good seasoned IT executive in a computer or an engineering discipline. Students today are being exposed to technologies far earlier than they were just 10 years ago. My son is in an engineering discipline in high school and will graduate with between 9 and 12 college credits as a result of the immersion in engineering.
- **Think about being a professor.** There are options for adjunct professors and full-time professors. An adjunct professor is great for CIOs who want to teach but not dedicate themselves completely in terms of time and effort.
- **Be a consultant.** CIOs are well poised for high IT strategy consulting positions. Look to the top national and international consulting organizations for possibilities.
- **Become a member of a board.** Joining either an advisory board or a full board of directors is a great way to leverage the significant experience of a CIO career. Advisory boards require less of a time commitment and in most cases offer no compensation. Full board positions are typically paid positions except in the nonprofit or academic sectors.
- **Become a mentor.** Mentoring is an important role for current and ex-executives as it's a great way to pass on knowledge and experience

to the next generation of leaders. I also firmly believe that CIOs today have an obligation to prepare the next generation of IT leaders for the challenges of tomorrow.

- **Retire and play golf.** For CIOs who *are* golfers, I need not say anything beyond *keep doing it*. Nongolfers should give it a try. Since the IT profession requires a high intellect, patience, teamwork, the ability to decipher complex technologies and solutions, accuracy, hard work, integrity, and a little bit of luck, golf may be just the thing for retiring executives.

I asked my IT executive advisory team for their insights on the next steps for a CIO. Their answers are in the CIO Survey below and, as usual, are insightful.

CIO SURVEY

What do you think is the next logical career step for a CIO?
What additional skills are required to get there?

- I think the CIO position lends itself to a number of career paths. Certainly in the right type of organization, the CIO might compete to be a CEO. Given the CIO's insights into the business processes and applications that support the organization, the COO role is probably a more natural next step than becoming a CEO. It is my experience that the CIO frequently knows as much or more about what is working or not "on the ground" from a process perspective in adjacent business units than even the responsibility executives. A successful CIO can also find opportunities as a consultant helping other CIOs become successful. A successful CIO spends a good deal of time "selling" internally and, in the correct situation, can make an effective transition into a sales or marketing role for technology providers they have used [in the past] and believe in.
—*John Sullivan, CIO, American Chemical Association*

- The [former] CIO of Indiana University is now the president. I think the CIO is well positioned to be the COO, since there are many overlapping skill sets and areas of knowledge. The CIO may have the broadest knowledge of any of the other senior officers. To lead a university, you need an advanced degree, usually a PhD.

- You need a track record of demonstrating success. [For ascension in the academic world] it would help if you have also been on both the administrative and academic side of the fence.

—*David Swartz, CIO, American University*

- The answer depends on the size of the company and the background of the CIO. In a small company in which the CIO has a technical background, the CIO would probably see the COO position as the next step. In a large company in which the CIO has a finance, engineering, or other business background, the next step could be anything, including the CEO position.

- Learn the numbers. The ability to influence, not manipulate. The ability to always do what is in the best interest of the business over your own personal interest. Those who have a passion for innovation. A little bit of insanity wouldn't hurt, either.

—*Earl Monsour, Director, Strategic Information Technologies, Maricopa Community College District*

- CEO, COO, and so forth. The scope of career progression possibilities for a CIO has broadened, and that includes the CEO position. These days, CIOs have increasingly varied backgrounds, and some use their CIO role to diversify their experience and progress within the organization.

- Having a thorough understanding of business, which is helpful in identifying opportunities, will make all of the difference within the organization. Having the will to take into account the needs of the employees and citizens when developing programs, the ability to understand their real needs, and the ability to decide to implement the appropriate technology solutions. Having the ability to make the connection between the technologies and the opportunities, in order to highlight the organization's market position.

—*Denis Garon, Associate with the Secretary of the Chief Information Secretariat of the Council of Treasury*

- The COO and CEO [roles are logical next steps] before retirement. How do you get there? Develop broad business acumen and prove you can think strategically and build great teams.

—*Joshua R. Jewett, SVP and CIO, Family Dollar Inc.*

What Did I Do to Prepare?

The following outlines what I've done in the last couple of years to plan for my next step:

- I've looked for opportunities where I can play a more strategic role than a tactical or an operating role.
- I've included other business executives (non-IT) from other sectors in my network to keep a dialogue running on other sectors and opportunities.
- I've aligned myself with several academic organizations and, when time permits, have put myself in front of a graduate-level class as an adjunct instructor.
- I've kept myself busy and current on both publications and presentations, domestic and global. Written and oral accomplishments contribute to one's brand.
- I recently signed up for a doctoral degree program to further my higher education in the hope that when I retire from IT, I can offer my services as a professor for the next decade or so. The caveat, though, is that my wife gets to pick the school because of all that she's endured from the IT profession and the time I've spent writing on weekends and evenings when we both preferred that I'd spent that time with the family instead of with my trusted computer.
- I've mapped out my future on paper and noted the skills required to get me there. Planning is key.

Recommendations

Preparing for the next role is an important part of anyone's career. I remember starting to plan for becoming a CIO while I was still in my twenties. Here I'm looking to offer insights and advice on what's possible for CIOs. In the end, what's both desirable and possible is most likely the winning combination. My recommendations are as follows:

- If you're not interested in retiring, look for strategic and innovative business opportunities and roles to complement your IT and operational skills.
- Read the full complement of information from Egon Zehnder International and research others like it to help prepare for a transformation from a CIO into another role: COO, CFO, or CEO. If you're not at the CIO level, see some of the following recommendations, especially concerning consulting and advisory boards.

- Seek out advisory and board positions that can further your opportunity for a transition beyond the role of IT and executive management. Nonprofit and educational institutions are great places to start, because they typically have great missions and provide the chance to give back to a worthy cause. For-profit boards offer financial compensation and, in many cases, stock.
- Consider becoming a strategic consultant or a research expert for the IT sector or for a key and interested vendor. I've often thought of moving into a cherished research analyst role at Forrester Research, IDC, or Gartner Research at some point in my career. It's a great way to leverage the expertise you've developed throughout your career and give to the next generation through seasoned advice and experience.
- Look for ways to give back to the IT sector. Mentoring, teaching, writing, and presenting are all viable options with a visibility that may lend itself to your next career move.
- If you're in a role that's not utilizing innovation and strategic thinking, consider *jumping* to your next opportunity.
- Spend time developing the end of your career path, as you did earlier in your career. Mapping out the skills, certifications, degrees, and relationships necessary to move to the next level will pay off in the end. Planning is the key to the beginning and end of one's career.

The IT profession continues to be one of the most exciting roles in the workforce. Today's business culture is rapidly changing and innovating. Businesses are using more technology than ever to meet their organizational and growth needs. Today's businesses are mobile, social, and cloud-based. To be competitive, you'll need to be in all three. Focus on retraining where appropriate; maintain important and helpful relationships with vendors, peers, and mentors; map out where you want to be in the next 5 to 10 years; and then make it happen.

Conclusion

The information technology industry continues to adapt, change, and come up with creative solutions and products to meet the changing climate and strategies associated with today's businesses, academic, and nonprofit organizations. IT professionals are contributing like never before to successes around the world and are being relied on more and more as the trends affecting the industry accelerate.

There are tremendous opportunities for today's IT professionals, whether they are analysts, system administrators, security professionals, network engineers, software developers, cloud professionals, SaaS providers, business intelligence and reporting experts, social media marketing specialists, telecommunications experts, trainers, infrastructure experts, or IT executives. Opportunities exist within organizations that consume technology and make decisions on mobile, social, and cloud computing as well as with the vendors that provide those services.

The industry remains robust. Keep learning new skills as the trends continue to evolve, and follow the money to know what trends are driving purchases. For those at the top, share your experiences with the next generation of IT leaders and become a mentor. The opportunities are endless. Never give up.

Notes

1. Samuel Johnson, Inspirational Quotes, www.inspirational-quotes.info/growth.html (accessed October 6, 2012).
2. Carrie Mathews, "What It Takes for a CIO to Be a CEO," *CIO*, June 25, 2007, www.cio.com/article/print/121151 (accessed August 5, 2012).
3. Ibid.
4. Ibid.

ABOUT THE AUTHOR

Gregory S. Smith has more than 25 years of IT experience. He currently serves as CIO for an international firm based in the Washington, D.C., area. Previously, he was the vice president and CIO for the World Wildlife Fund (WWF) in Washington, D.C. Prior to working at WWF, Smith directed software development, e-business, and business intelligence activities for AARP in Washington, D.C. Before that, he was with Sallie Mae, a Fortune 200 financial services firm, where he directed technology for the Corporate Finance Division and two subsidiaries. He has also served as a principal consultant in the Management Consulting Solutions group at PricewaterhouseCoopers LLP and as a defense IT consultant for SRA International.

Smith is a recipient of the following awards: *SmartCEO* magazine's Top 10 CIOs in Washington, D.C., in 2011; *Computer World* magazine's Premier 100 IT Leaders, in 2007; *CIO* magazine's CIO 100, in 2003; and *eWeek* magazine's Top 100 CIOs, in 2007. He is the author of *Protecting Your Children on the Internet: A Road Map for Parents and Teachers* (Praeger, 2009) and *Straight to the Top: Becoming a World-Class CIO* (John Wiley & Sons, 2006). He has published many articles in his career, including "Talking at the Top of the World" in *CIO* magazine.

Smith received a B.S. in computer science from the University of Maryland at College Park and an M.S. in business from Johns Hopkins University, where he also served for 15 years as an adjunct faculty member in the Carey Business School graduate programs.

Smith can be contacted through his web site, www.gregoryssmith.com.

INDEX